InternQube

Professional Skills for the Workplace

Michael True

First edition, 2011 © INTRUEITION, LLC
Second edition, 2013 © INTRUEITION, LLC
Third edition, 2018 © INTRUEITION, LLC

True, Michael.
    InternQube: Professional Skills for the Workplace
    by Michael True
        ISBN 978-0-9890918-1-7
        Subject headings—
            Experiential learning--United States--Hand
                books, manuals, etc.
            Education, Higher--United States.
            School-to-work transition.
            Education, Cooperative--United States--Hand
                books, manuals, etc.
            Internships

Cover and Layout Design: Lindsay M. Attaway,
butashadow.com

Printed and bound in the United States
INTRUEITION.com

DEDICATION

This book is dedicated to all who value experiential learning. May this book help to move you toward professionalism, growth, and success.

TABLE OF CONTENTS

Introduction – Your Adventure

Chapters

Quick Notes

Blournal – Questions for Reflection
Recommendations

INTRODUCTION – YOUR ADVENTURE

After having taken numerous classes on campus, you wisely decided to experience the world of work. You probably spoke with your advisor and with the Career or Internship Center. Plans were set forth, potential organizations researched, resumes sent, interviews conducted, and a choice made.

Gaining practical work experience related to your career goal is no longer an option. It is a critically important part of one's education. The benefits you can reap from an internship or co-op experience are numerous and include broad areas such as academics, personal growth, and professional development. You have made an excellent decision and are, therefore, to be congratulated! This work-integrated learning experience may be the key, which will unlock the door to a job or acceptance into the next phase of your education.

Joseph Campbell, author of *The Hero With A Thousand Faces*, demonstrated that stories of "the hero's journey" throughout time and across cultures have the same basic elements – departure, initiation, and return. You, too, are going on a type of hero's journey. You are about to depart, or have already done so. In the process, you will most likely leave your familiar home (campus), become initiated into the world of work with its challenges, and return to campus transformed in thinking and behavior. When you return, you will view your classes, textbooks, and assignments differently. You will, no doubt, want to bring change to your future learning experiences.

You are embarking upon an adventure. There will be people and resources along the way to assist you. One very modest attempt to help you develop professional skills is this book. It is simple to understand and written in a "get to the point" kind of way. Several topics in the following chapters have had many books written about them. The tactic used here is not to reproduce everything that has been written or said or recorded about a particular topic. It is to present the heart, or core, of what you need to know to make that subject useful for your development. Chapters are short and to the point.

You may look at several subjects as "no brainers". If you see much of this as common sense and already within your realm of understanding, you are to be applauded. However, considering recent surveys of employers across the country, they are not seeing these abilities applied in the workplace. Don't allow this to be just head knowledge. Use what you learn.

This text is one tool to be used for a meaningful experience. Many factors will come into play, including your own inner motivation and desire to do well. Also, the effort that your site and supervisor put into your experience will play a crucial role. And don't forget there are resources waiting at your school - the wisdom of faculty and career/internship coaches, and their libraries and websites which are loaded with useful information.

We'll start with a basic orientation to your internship. Then we'll move into areas that virtually every student faces at some point during the internship experience. These will include subjects such as understanding organizational culture, working with your supervisor and co-workers, dealing with workplace issues including stress and office politics, virtual internships, personal branding, and more.

Last, but not least, be sure to use the many resources of **InternQube.com** – the free, companion website to this book.

MAKING THE MOST OF YOUR INTERNSHIP

Managing the Immediate
You need to think about how the internship is affecting you and the relationships with those around you. If, as is the case with many interns, you are working at your internship site while also taking classes on campus, you may feel at times like you are living two lives. You have one foot on campus and one foot in the pre-professional world of work. Because of this, you may feel strains developing with your roommates. If you are interning full-time and aren't taking classes, you may find other issues developing.

Those around you may wonder why you can't stay up as late as you used to, or why you can't spend time participating in activities that were once part of everyday life. It will help to sit down with your roommate or with those in your apartment and explain your current situation. Stepping into the professional world has implications. You need your sleep to function as needed at your site. Money may become an issue, as you need to save it for transportation to and from your site. Time management becomes ever more crucial, especially if projects need to be worked on outside of your internship environment.

Thinking About the Long Term
Remember, this internship is at once about you...and not about you. You are in this experience to grow personally and pro-

fessionally, get a good reference, and improve your chances for success in future jobs and/or graduate school. But you are also representing members of your family, the school you come from, and your religious belief system, if you have one. Just as you observe others and make judgments, so people at your internship are listening to your words and observing your behavior. Based on what they see and hear, they are making judgments about what and whom you represent. For instance, if you  do well at your internship, your site and supervisor may very well want to host other students from your institution. You have the ability to open doors for future students, or close them by your poor behavior or performance. So think about the implications with respect to the longer term and wider life issues of your work/learning experience. You are sowing seeds for the future.

You are sowing seeds for the future.

Expectations

What we expect from a person, place, or event can easily affect our level of satisfaction when we actually meet or experience them. You may wonder what's around the next bend on this internship journey. For example, if you go to a concert and have high expectations for the performer(s) to behave in a certain way and to sing certain songs, but they don't, you will most likely walk away disappointed. If, however, you manage your expectations based upon reports of others who have attended previous concerts or by an account you've read about a previous event, you will probably go home satisfied.

What are you expecting from your work site and your supervisor? Do you even know who your supervisor will be? Do you have a clear job or position description, which details the work you will be doing? Obtaining a description provides a lens through which you can manage your expectations. With a clear position description and what was communicated during the interview (assuming you had one), your expectations should be realistic.

But don't get the idea that expectations are a one-way street. What do you think your supervisor and co-workers are expecting from you? Based on the school you are attending, or the professors they know you have had, your past work or travels, your family upbringing, or the recommendations of others, they may have any number of expectations. You may want to ask your supervisor and co-workers this question during the first week or two of your internship. It may help to clear up any preconceived notions you and they may have.

People like to work with others who have an overall good attitude toward life.

Attitude

Your attitude makes all the difference in the world. People like to work with others who have an overall good attitude toward life. No one likes to work with a grouch. How can you develop a positive attitude?

A great start is to begin your day by identifying people and/or circumstances for which you are thankful. Some of them may seem insignificant; others may hold great importance in your life. Whatever they may be, express your gratefulness before your day moves into "rush" mode.

Science has discovered an interesting phenomenon. Inner emotions influence what is seen on a person's face, but the opposite is true as well. Facial expression alone can affect your autonomic nervous system. If you have a scowl or an angry look on your face, your heart rate and body temperature will increase. If you smile, even if you don't feel like it, a positive physiological reaction begins to occur in your body. For more on this read pp. 206-208 in Malcolm Gladwell's book, *Blink*. So…smile. The benefits will help you and positively influence others.

Another way to help develop a positive attitude is to find ways to serve others. You may discover people in need at work, or in your apartment complex, or through volunteering at a community organization. Serving others in their need helps to frame your own problems in a more realistic way, and it helps to curb your ego and narcissistic tendencies.

Daily Conduct
The following short list isn't meant for you to be obsessive about, but they are some things to keep in mind:
- Don't go to work having just rolled out of bed. Shower, shave, brush your teeth and gargle, if necessary, before heading out.
- Be careful how much perfume or cologne you put on.
- Keep jewelry to a minimum.
- Do not wear any body piercings.
- Clothing should be clean and pressed, and shoes should be clean and shined (if leather).
- Dress for the position you want, not the one you currently have.
- Keep your language "clean" and avoid crude jokes or stories.
- Do not surf the web in your free time; use your time wisely to learn new aspects of your job or what others do in the organization.
- Do not post anything - photos or text - about your site on Facebook or any other social networking website.
- Keep personal information to yourself; don't let your life become the office soap opera.
- Be friendly; make an extra effort to get along with people.
- Be positive and supportive; make others look good whenever possible.

- Keep an open mind; avoid jumping to conclusions; try to make informed judgments.
- Follow through - cover every angle of a project and be accurate.
- Be appropriately assertive - don't go into the experience with a "know-it-all" attitude, but don't go in thinking you have nothing to offer either.

Conducting yourself in a professional manner on a daily basis will have many positive ramifications. At the very least, it will aid you when the time comes for you to ask for a letter(s) of reference. Most of all, it will speak volumes about who you are to all with whom you come in contact. They will quickly learn you are a serious "professional in training".

Time Management
Managing the time you have available becomes more crucial each day.

- Research indicates that for every hour of planning, you save three or four hours of work, so plan and prioritize tomorrow's commitments today.
- Start your day by arriving a few minutes early to get yourself settled in before your world gets hectic.
- Know your rhythms and blues. What part of the day is best for you? If possible, tackle the difficult issues or people when you are at your peak.
- Be disciplined and stay current with a single time management device.
- Use a digital or paper system to remind you of important deadlines.

Networking
Networking is simply establishing a link with another person(s). Building a professional network is very important. Though you may not wish to believe it, the old adage is often true – "It's

not what you know, but who you know that counts." You need to have a vibrant skill set and a solid educational background. When those are combined with a continuously growing network of professional contacts, you increase your chances of being offered new opportunities.

Plug Into Professional Activities
- Talk with your supervisor about making the most of your internship.
- Ask to attend trade shows, conferences, professional meetings and lunches.
- Develop contacts. Identify yourself as an intern seeking to learn more about the profession. Most people will enjoy sharing their background and experience.
- Find out what the trends are in your chosen profession. By doing so, you may gain a clearer idea of the path you wish to pursue.

Test The Feasibility Of A Pet Project/Idea
If you have a particular activity or experience you want to try, don't hesitate to ask if you can pursue it, especially if it fits into your overall job description and supports your learning objective(s). Remember, however, your idea may have been tried by the department or organization at some point in the past, so be tactful in your approach to the topic. You may wish to say something like, "This may have already been tried, but I was wondering if it would be helpful to…"

Value of Setting Goals
"First say to yourself what you would be; and then do what you have to do." – Epictetus

David Allen writes about the importance of setting goals for work and larger life issues on pp. 46-47 of his book, *Ready for Anything*.

"I am continually amazed at how often I forget about our astonishing ability to create what we want by what we envision. Outcome thinking and a willingness to visualize something's being true before it's physically present is a master skill that we all could probably develop to a much greater degree. I just looked at a mind map I did 10 years ago. It was about what I wanted my life to be like, if I could really have it the way I wanted it. In my apartment, with a set of colored pens, it took me a couple of hours to fill in the whole page, drawing little pictures and putting into words and phrases as I was moved to do so. The vision was a big one. It included how I wanted to be working, what kind of freedom and resources I would have, what successes I would be achieving, and various aspects of a desirable lifestyle - even what my inner life would be like. I can't say that it's all come to pass, but when I looked at the drawing and then looked at my current life, I saw how all those images for years had sparked and supported my significant choices...much of the little mural was quite exact about what has come to pass."

"Goals are dreams with deadlines." - Diana Scharf Hunt

"The reason most people never reach their goals is that they don't define them, or ever seriously consider them as believable or achievable. Winners can tell you where they are going, what they plan to do along the way, and who will be sharing the adventure with them." - Denis Waitley, Ph.D.

Learning Goals/Objectives

Unless you are required to do so, you may not even think about writing out some learning objectives. Take time to work through the process below and develop some. They serve as your strategic plan for what you intend to learn during the internship experience. They form a written agreement negotiated between you, your internship advisor and your work supervisor. A written plan helps you direct, manage and reflect upon the learning process.

Each objective you formulate should have the following components:
- Learning Objective: What it is that I want to learn?
- Activities/Resources: How am I going to learn it?
- Evaluation/Verification: How am I going to demonstrate what I learned?

Begin with a perspective that you are making a contract with yourself. You are identifying what knowledge, behavior, competencies, attitudes and values you wish to develop. These learning objectives are your plan (not your site supervisor's, nor your internship advisor's, nor your parent's). The objectives outline how you will attempt to reach your goals and when you will know that you have reached them.

Brainstorm responses to the following general questions:
- "What do I most want to explore, understand or learn during my internship?"
- "How would I like to change or be different by the end of this experience?"
- "What will make me more marketable to an employer or graduate school?"

Once you have developed a list of possible objectives, review the list and try to prioritize them. Which ones are most important to you? Do the objectives support academic, professional, and personal concerns? After you have selected one or more key objectives, talk them over with your site supervisor and your campus faculty or internship/co-op coordinator. Review them regularly to be sure you are on course to fulfill them.

Document Completed Objectives

You will put a lot of work into your experience, so be sure to document the fulfillment of your learning objectives and the good things you have done at your site. This may involve putting together an executive summary of your work – a concise document about three pages in length. You may also wish to create a portfolio which includes samples of your work – research, writing, newsletters, event brochures, screen shots of databases or spreadsheets, photos, illustrations, a letter from your supervisor attesting to your accomplishments in a particular area of work, etc. The portfolio may be presented to employers and graduate schools in a variety of media, but the preferred medium for many is a website. Be sure to read the chapter on Personal Branding and Transitioning to Employment.

Value of Feedback and Evaluation

You will know you are making progress toward your goals, if you honestly examine yourself and have someone else, like your work supervisor, evaluate you. Try to set up a specified time each week when you can meet with your site supervisor for his/her feedback about your work thus far, to help you plan for upcoming projects, and to obtain their advice in areas where you realize you are weak.

No doubt you will hear some good feedback on your performance. You may also hear some constructive criticism about areas where your performance needs to improve. Don't be upset. Thank your supervisor for being honest and helpful. Reflect on that feedback and focus on doing better in those areas.

Stages of an Internship

As with any new employee, interns proceed through certain stages of adjustment in order to become oriented to the organization, before becoming a fully functioning member of that group.

If you understand the stages you are likely to pass through as an intern, then you can more effectively deal with a variety of situations at the worksite.

Entry

During this stage which may last anywhere from a few days to two weeks, you will probably find that:
- the office routine, procedures and people are new
- it works best to go slowly; don't try to learn everything at once
- you're allowed to ask "dumb" questions
- this is the only time you will see things as a client or customer would on a first visit, so be sure to write down your initial thoughts and impressions of the site and your co-workers
- bridges with co-workers begin to be built
- you are shown how to do things, without necessarily being asked to do them
- you are learning the ropes, so mistakes are expected and tolerated
- emotions you experience include eagerness, hope, and anxiety

Initiation

This stage usually lasts from one to four weeks and is marked by:
- increasing expectations with regard to your work performance
- more critical reviews of your work, as well as praise
- a tendency on your part to overreact to negative comments, but don't take them personally
- greater insight into the organization's "culture"
- co-workers trying to draw you into office politics; try to remain neutral
- emotions which may include disillusionment and tension

Competency
This stage, which should happen by about the sixth week, will find you:
- no longer asking "Can I do it?" but "How will I do it?"
- beginning to raise questions. You may see possible solutions to problems, but you don't have the authority to do a great deal about them
- becoming more of a participant, but try to maintain a balance between that role and that of an observer
- feeling more confident of your abilities, role, and place in the organization

Completion
The time of your departure draws near. You now need to focus on:
- assessing and reevaluating yourself and your career
- concluding your experience well, including saying "thank you" to your supervisor and co-workers in meaningful and appropriate ways
- final exams, or graduation, or entry-level employment
- working through the emotions of relief or sadness

Personal Qualities Needed In All Stages
Throughout your work/learning experience you should exhibit qualities such as:
- seeking to work well with a team of people
- humility as you complete assignments and deal with a variety of co-workers
- empathy - a sense of concern for co-workers and their struggles, since they will remain in that setting after you have completed your internship
- an appropriate assertiveness
- a good work ethic; that is, be willing to go above and beyond what is expected

Best wishes for a successful work/learning experience!

RISK AWARENESS AND MANAGEMENT

Essentially, risk management is concerned with the outcome of future events that cannot be predicted with certainty, and how to handle this uncertainty.

There are four basic steps in being aware of, and managing, risk.
1. Identify Potential Risks
2. Understand Guidelines and Expectations from the College and Employer Perspectives
3. Consider Solutions to Potential Problems
4. Inform Your Campus Internship Coordinator of Any Concern

Should an incident take place:
1. Be sure to document all facts such as date, time, persons involved, and the situation as you observed it.
2. Inform your supervisor and/or your campus internship coordinator immediately.

The following areas may seem like common sense and a normal part of life. However, it is at those times when these matters are not considered, or thought through, that something happens, and we are at a loss as to how to proceed.

This list is in no way comprehensive. It is meant as a stimulus for you to reflectively examine your internship environment and circumstances.

Travel
- To and from the site – consider dangerous intersections, streets or stretches of highway
- Parking garages or poorly lit parking areas
- Using your car, or a vehicle provided for you, for organization business. Find out all policies dealing with areas such as:
  ○ Reimbursement of funds expended out of your pocket
  ○ Transporting clients
  ○ Transporting sensitive or easily-damaged materials
  ○ Transporting potentially hazardous materials

Physical Hazards
- Working outdoors – sun, snow and ice, other extreme weather, pollution, power lines, pipelines, gas lines, microwave equipment, electromagnetic radiation
- Working indoors – any type of machinery, large and/or heavy objects, unsuitable working conditions such as extreme temperatures, asbestos, "sick building" odors, insecure buildings where there may be structural concerns, closed off or blocked fire escapes, etc.

Biological Hazards
- Animals, birds, or fish you may work with/upon, dead or alive, and possible transmission of infections - e.g., Mad Cow disease, West Nile virus and bird flu
- Poisonous plants

Chemical Hazards
- Water supply – e.g., high levels of lead
- Toner powders from laser printer cartridges or photocopiers – eye or lung irritation
- Chemicals in a laboratory setting – eyes, open sores, inhalation

Interpersonal Hazards

- Harassment
  - ○ Inform yourself of the site sponsor's harassment policy and follow it, should one exist.
  - ○ Sexual, age, ethnic, racial, religious, or disability harassment of student workers, or any employee, is illegal.
  - ○ The employer must insure that regular, full-time employees, or other interns, do not harass student workers.
  - ○ Immediately report any harassment to your campus internship coordinator.
  - ○ Situations will be handled in accordance with your campus policy.
  - ○ Resolution may include placing you in another position or removing you from the site.
  - ○ Harassment of others by you in the workplace may result in your dismissal from the program.
- Sexual Assault
  - ○ Set limits; don't give mixed messages.
  - ○ Trust your "gut feeling" or intuition about situations to avoid.
  - ○ Be clear and responsible in your communication with others.
  - ○ If necessary, be forceful, firm, and assertive in your communication with others.
  - ○ Be aware of nonverbal cues that can alert you to a problem.
  - ○ Remember, silence is not consent.
  - ○ Don't assume the other person knows what you do or do not want.
  - ○ Use the buddy system...watch out for your friends.
  - ○ Don't lose control- alcohol and other drugs affect your judgment.
  - ○ Avoid secluded places.

- Do not assume that, if you are with a friend or an acquaintance, nothing bad will happen.

- Devise an action plan in advance for what you will do if confronted with a situation of possible acquaintance rape. Remove yourself from the situation at the first sign that you are feeling controlled or unsafe.

- Become comfortable with the idea that you might have to be rude, make noise, yell, etc. to remove yourself from a possible sexual assault situation. Do not worry about hurting the other person.

- An excellent, comprehensive website, with numerous helpful links, is provided by the University of North Carolina - Greensboro : *https://tinyurl.com/y973f7ka*

Harassment Policies and Procedures

Your school is committed to engaging students in professional and safe working/learning environments. Any form of harassment, intimidation or discrimination related to skin color, race (and related physical characteristics), gender, cultural heritage, ethnicity and nationality should not be tolerated. This applies to site supervisors and co-workers toward a student, as well as students toward their site supervisors and co-workers.

Misconduct of Supervisor/Co-Workers Towards a Student Intern

You should inform yourself of the site sponsor's sexual harassment policy and follow it, should one exist. Beyond this, you should report any incident as soon as possible to your campus internship coordinator, allowing both the school and the internship site the opportunity to promptly intervene.

Behaviors that may constitute sexual harassment include (but are not limited to) the following:

- subtle pressure for sexual activity
- unnecessary brushes or touches

- offensive sexual graffiti
- disparaging remarks about one's gender
- physical aggression such as pinching and patting
- sexual innuendos or persistent use of sexually suggestive language which another person finds offensive, demeaning, or otherwise inappropriate
- verbal sexual abuse disguised as humor
- obscene gestures
- sexist remarks about a person's clothing, body, or sexual activities
- conditioning an educational or employment decision or benefit on submission to sexual conduct

Misconduct of Student Intern Towards a Supervisor/Co-Workers

Most instances of misconduct are directed toward students, but there are a few situations in which student interns misbehave towards a supervisor or co-workers. In these cases, schools request site supervisors to report any incident as soon as possible allowing the school the opportunity to promptly intervene. These interventions may include a variety of responses, including removing you from your internship site.

VIRTUAL INTERNSHIPS – CHECKLIST FOR SUCCESS

A virtual internship provides the opportunity for students to work from any location at any time using various forms of technology. Interns do not need to be at a specific physical site with one or more co-workers. Occasional interactions may take place face-to-face, but most will occur using digital devices, due to their ubiquity and ease of use.

Advantages
1. No need to relocate
2. Often allows for flexible work hours
3. Allows for casual dress except for formal presentations (see the chapter on Virtual Meetings),
4. Those who are more introverted may gain a greater sense of empowerment through online work

Disadvantages
1. Possible lack of quality supervision
2. More difficult to understand organizational culture and to make sense of office "politics"
3. Difficult if you are not a self-starter and need a lot of interaction and instruction
4. Most likely must use your own hardware and sometimes your own software

To ensure the best possible chance of success use the following checklist:

☐ The organization should be an established, legitimate business or non-profit, as evidenced by having –
- a physical location
- website
- history of offering paid employment
- listed telephone number
- tax ID number

☐ If the organization consists of a single individual, are they willing to show you results of their criminal background check?

☐ The organization must agree to offer an experience that meets the criteria of a legitimate internship as outlined by the National Association of Colleges and Employers:
- The experience must be an extension of the classroom: a learning experience that provides for applying the knowledge gained in the classroom. It must not be simply to advance the operations of the employer or be the work that a regular employee would routinely perform.
- The skills or knowledge learned must be transferable to other employment settings.
- The experience has a defined beginning and end, and a job description with desired qualifications.
- There are clearly defined learning objectives related to the student's professional goals.
- There is supervision by a professional with expertise and educational and/or professional background in the field of the experience.
- There is routine feedback by the experienced supervisor.
- There are resources, equipment, and facilities provided by the host employer that support learning objectives/goals.

☐ You and the organization, with approval of your campus

internship coordinator, need to agree on a clear, detailed position description, which covers all expectations and constitutes a successful internship.

☐ The organization's internship site mentor must provide you with regular supervision, mentoring, and feedback as outlined above. This will include:

- Use of a company intranet or virtual workspace on a server, or an online project management or document-sharing tool, such as Office 365, Google Docs, or a similar program. This will allow the supervisor to go online and monitor the work to be completed. The work is stored in the "cloud," not on a single PC, so it is always available to those who need it.
- A regularly scheduled email report in which you provide information to the internship site mentor and the academic advisor, such as hours worked, challenges or problems encountered, progress toward learning objectives, and any questions you may have.
- A weekly virtual meeting on Skype, GMail video chat or a similar technology to provide more personalized feedback to you.
- If the virtual internship is within a reasonable drive from your campus, the employer needs to meet with you in a public place (e.g., coffee shop, restaurant) once a week. This face-to-face meeting is a time for project planning, review of progress made, feedback, and mentoring.

☐ The organization should make you part of regular operations as much as possible; for example, including you in face-to-face opportunities such as company meetings or client visits.

☐ The organization must be willing to host a site visit from a representative of the college.

□ You should be able to provide your faculty advisor or internship coordinator with materials produced during your experience.

Adapted from a personal document and modified by professional colleagues on the Internship-Net listserv.

(Special thanks to Rich Grant, Career Development Educator, for synthesizing my work with contributions from our Internship-Net listserv colleagues.)

WHAT EMPLOYERS WANT

Employer expectations have increased for interns and entry-level employees. The marketplace is changing at an ever-quickening pace, and a new era of work is upon us. Organizations need people who can onboard quickly and hit the ground running.

There are several sources of data on what types of skills employers are looking for now and in the coming years. Two excellent sources that look at human capital worldwide are the World Economic Forum and Deloitte. They view the workplace landscape broadly and take into account many companies throughout the world representing millions of employees.

The World Economic Forum speaks of a rapidly approaching Fourth Industrial Revolution in this way. "The First Industrial Revolution used water and steam power to mechanize production. The Second used electric power to create mass production. The Third used electronics and information technology to automate production. Now a Fourth Industrial Revolution is building on the Third, the digital revolution that has been occurring since the middle of the last century. It is characterized by a fusion of technologies that is blurring the lines between the physical, digital, and biological spheres." - The Fourth Industrial Revolution: What it Means, How to Respond

Deloitte writes in their Global Human Capital Trends Report

that "The impact of the fourth industrial revolution is fundamentally changing the nature of work and the meaning of career, and making it imperative to constantly refresh one's skills." This means you need to take advantage of resources like those found at Lynda.com, a division of LinkedIn, which has training related to almost every one of the skills listed below.

The World Economic Forum has compiled an excellent list. These align with reports from other sources that are strictly North America-based. The top ten skills needed now and in the coming years are

1. Complex Problem Solving
2. Critical Thinking
3. Creativity
4. People Management
5. Coordinating with Others
6. Emotional Intelligence
7. Judgment / Decision Making
8. Service Orientation
9. Negotiation
10. Cognitive Flexibility

Each of these skills needs to be explored in depth through various media. Some of them are addressed elsewhere in this book. Besides Lynda.com, check online resources like Udacity.com, Coursera.org, MindTools.com, and other channels through which you can potentially earn certificates by proving your competencies. Certificates, badges, and other forms of proof of competency in specific skills are increasingly required.

Of course, the best way to learn and test these skills is through direct, hands-on experience through an internship. So, you're already ahead of the competition. Talk with your site supervisor about ways to develop a few of these during your time with the organization. Use them as a basis for creating or enhancing your learning objectives.

ORGANIZATIONAL CULTURE

Everyone is unique. Each of us has a distinctive DNA code that shapes aspects of who we are. The people, places, circumstances, and events of our upbringing are different. These, along with choices we make about where we live, what we eat, the type of work we do, the types of music we listen to, the people with whom we associate, and much more, shape us into matchless individuals. All of these factors help form our personality.

Organizations are not much different. Each one has a set of characteristics that are woven together to make it a unique place to work. History, traditions, philosophy, values, management, and current employees blend together to form an organization's culture – its personality, if you will. To work well within an organization, you need to understand and appreciate its culture.

Components of culture you need to reflect upon include the following:

Purpose of the organization
- What is the organization trying to achieve?
- Why does it exist?
- Does the organization have a stated mission?

Philosophy
- What person or document is the guiding light of the orga-

nization?
- How does the organization conduct business?
- What parameters are placed on the strategies used to achieve its goals?

Values
- What beliefs or credos exist?
- Is the organization fiscally conservative or liberal?
- Do a majority of the employees tend to support a specific political party?
- Are certain traditions observed?
- Is there a "hero" who is celebrated for his/her past or current performance?

Behavioral Expectations and Limits
- Does the organization tell you how to behave in certain situations?
- Does it extend these expectations into your personal life?
- Does the organization encourage conformance or does it tolerate mavericks?

Attitudes of Employees
- What do the employees talk about?
- Are they happy and motivated or down and lethargic?
- Power hungry or mutually supportive?

Work Ethic
- Do people go above and beyond in their commitment to projects?
- What role does work play in their lives?

Dress Code
- Do men wear a suit and tie or dress casually?
- Do women wear dresses and suits or something less formal?

Character of the Organization
- Is the organization stodgy and sluggish or vibrant and bustling?
- Centralized or decentralized?
- Entrepreneurial or bureaucratic?

Social Norms
- Does the organization require certain types of social obligations and/or behavior from you?
- Do you have to belong to certain clubs or socialize in the right places?
- Are you expected to attend informal gatherings frequently?
- Do employees socialize together often?

Management Norms
- How are the employees managed?
- Are managers autocratic or democratic?
- How much, and what type, of control is exercised over people?
- How would you have to behave to best get along with your boss?

Atmosphere
- Are people relaxed and happy or formal and on edge?
- Is there an atmosphere of trust or fear?

Career Progression and Success
- How do people progress through their careers?
- Is progression largely seniority-based, or is it results-based?
- Is movement across functional areas encouraged?
- What are the characteristics of the high-level successful people?

Strategic Orientation
- Does management have a clearly outlined strategy?

- Is its thinking short-term or long-term?

Ethical Standards
- Is there a strong ethical orientation in the company?
- Are people concerned about honesty and fairness in business?
- Is there a sense of broader social responsibility?

Political Environment
- To what extent is organizational politics a factor in accomplishing tasks?
- Who holds power and how do they use it?
- Do different parts of the organization work together well, or is there a strong sense of "protecting one's turf"?
- Which is more important: who you know or what you do?

Communication
- Do people talk openly and freely, or are discussions guarded?
- Are communication lines formal, progressing through layers of the organization?
- Or do you see top management talking regularly with lower levels of the organization?
- To what extent does management keep employees informed about the company's progress?

Think about your organization. Reflect on these questions. The faster you grasp the culture of your internship or co-op site, the easier it will be to maneuver through it and to make progress on the work assigned to you.

FIRST IMPRESSIONS

Nothing happens faster than first impressions. When initially meeting someone, you need to manage the impression you leave with other people.

This was clearly demonstrated when a Harvard University psychology professor did an experiment with one of her first-year classes. She showed her students a video recording of another professor; someone none of them had yet taken for a class. This was no ordinary viewing experience, however. The video clip was only ten seconds in length, and the audio was muted. The students saw the professor teaching a class for only ten seconds without any sound.

They were then given an end-of-semester evaluation form and asked to rate the professor they had just watched for ten seconds. Individually, they went through category after category. The rating forms were collected and tabulated. Can you guess the results? Those psychology students who saw, and did not hear, that professor for only ten seconds rated him the same as students who sat under his teaching for a full semester. That is the power of first impressions!

Most often the first impression people receive is visual. Be careful with your appearance. Having observed workers at your site during the interview process, or what was communicated to you by human resources or your site supervisor, you should dress accordingly. If your interview was by phone, be sure to dress on the conservative side for your first appearance on site. Your clothes should be clean and pressed, and your shoes should be clean and shined.

Ask yourself, "What am I communicating by my appearance?" You want people to pay attention to your words and the ideas you express, not to your clothing or hair, or accessories. Your supervisor and co-workers should be focusing on your face and what you are saying. If their eyes are looking anywhere else, you need to consider your clothing. Is it too tight? Too low cut? Or is it distracting in some other way? If so, do yourself a favor and change how you dress. Help others to maintain their focus on your good words, creative ideas, and positive work performance.

> *Anything, which diverts a person's attention away from your words or the good work you do, may be detrimental to your professional success.*

Your hair should not be distracting either. This goes for women and men. You should not need to constantly push your hair back over your ears or fling it back to keep it out of your eyes. Hair can be just as distracting as certain types of clothing. Anything which diverts a person's attention away from your words, or the good work you do, may be detrimental to your professional success.

Nametags may become a part of your professional life. If you are given one at your worksite, or at a meeting, luncheon, or a professional function, you need to know where to place it. Though a nametag will have your name on it, it isn't about you. It is there for others to put a name with a face. That is why a nametag should be placed on the upper right lapel. When you shake hands with someone, their eye will travel up your right arm to the nametag and your face, back to the nametag, and then back again to your face. Your nametag is there as a courtesy to those you meet.

After the initial visual impression of your appearance, you will probably be judged on your handshake. There are a few different kinds.

- The Limp Fish – the hand is extremely weak. The impression one receives is that you lack confidence.
- The Bone Crusher – grabbing a person's hand and squeezing hard. The impression is you are overconfident and aggressive.
- The Firm Hand – not too strong, but not weak - placing the web (between your thumb and forefinger) of your right hand into the web of the other person's right hand. Confidence and poise are the good impressions you will leave.

If you're prone to sweaty palms, wipe your hand on the inside of your pant pocket, or on the leg of your pants or skirt prior to shaking a person's hand. It's not the best solution, but it may help you.

Speaking is the next way people will form an impression of you. Do you use good vocabulary? Do you enunciate your words well? Do you speak with appropriate volume for the setting in which you find yourself? If you don't pay attention to these components of speech, your audience may be looking at you, but they won't be paying attention to what you're saying.

Other aspects of first impressions are body piercings and tattoos. Your internship site may not approve of, or have restrictions regarding, piercings and tattoos. Remove piercings and cover tattoos as best as possible. Err on the conservative side until you learn they are approved, appropriate at your site, and accepted by co-workers.

Finally, be sure to practice good hygiene. Bathe each day. Do not go to your internship having just rolled out of bed. No one wants to be introduced to, or work beside, a person who smells like sleep, or something worse. Also, be careful to not overuse cologne or perfume.

PROCESSING YOUR EXPERIENCES

We experience a host of people and circumstances each and every day. But do we learn from what we experience? At the heart of it, we need to want to learn. Hopefully, you have a desire to learn everything about your worksite, the people, and all that takes place there. Beyond the initial desire to want to learn, we need to be observant.

We have been given two eyes and two ears, but only one mouth. Why is it, then, that we often talk more than we observe with our eyes and our ears? From Sherlock Holmes to Patrick Jane in *The Mentalist*, great detectives in literature, movies and television use keen powers of observation. Sherlock Holmes is the quintessential model of a keen observer. His assistant said, "Holmes, you see everything." Holmes responded, "I see no more than you, but I have trained myself to **notice** what I see." – Adventure of the Blanched Soldier by Conan Doyle. Have we trained ourselves to truly notice what we see and what we hear? For an interesting look at what we don't really notice, search YouTube for "Derren Brown Tricks Advertisers With Subliminal Messaging."

After noticing someone or something, the next step is to gather facts. A simple, helpful guide is to ask yourself six questions and put the gathered facts in those categories. The six questions are tried and true – Who? What? When? Where? Why? and How? By cataloguing your facts with these questions, you begin the process of reflection, which is where deep learning occurs. Now, take these facts and arrange them into a "picture" of what you have experienced.

The following are just a few insights from an article entitled 'Organizing For Learning: A New Imperative' by Dr. Peter Ewell.

• Cognitive science tells us the brain's activity is in direct proportion to its engagement with actively stimulating environments.

• Maximum learning tends to occur when people are confronted with specific, identifiable problems with which to work.

• Brain research tells us that a challenge produces major surges in short-term neural activity. But building lasting cognitive connections requires considerable periods of reflection. Absent reflection, solving presenting problems usually ends learning encounters at a point well short of the cognitive reorganization that deep learning requires. Effective learning situations require time for thinking.

Using the Lewin/Kolb Experiential Learning Model (*Experiential Learning: Experience as The Source of Learning and Development* by David A. Kolb), which is shown on the following page, diagram and write comments about an incident or event that occurs during your internship experience. This could be something in which you are directly involved or something you witness. What lessons or conclusions can you draw from it?

This process happens many times every day, but we don't think about it. A very simple example, which can happen in a matter of seconds, is this.

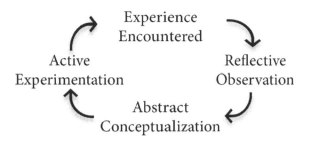

1. Experience Encountered - You are introduced to a person for the first time. You shake hands and notice the palm of her right hand is a bit sweaty.
2. Reflective Observation – You note she seems a bit unsure of herself. She finds it difficult to maintain good eye contact.
3. Abstract Conceptualization – You surmise she lacks confidence in this new setting. Maybe she is very qualified for the project, but just has a difficult time when first meeting new people. To help her feel relaxed, you decide to offer her something to drink, offer her a deserved compliment, and/or talk to her about a non-threatening subject.
4. Active Experimentation – You carry through on your conceptualization and find that she makes better eye contact, smiles, and seems to relax a bit.

Take time to observe and notice, ask yourself the six key questions, organize your answers, look for connections between them, and utilize the Lewin/Kolb Model. If you apply yourself to this process, your learning will be deeper, fuller, and richer. You will also find yourself developing stronger abilities in problem solving.

UNDERSTANDING AND WORKING WITH YOUR SUPERVISOR

Your supervisor is a human being with all the joys, sorrows, stresses and opportunities that come with life. He or she is not superhuman, nor are they perfect in any sense of the word. They supervise one or more individuals, and no doubt have one or more people to whom they report. They are neither your friend, nor your enemy. Their work is not their life, even though some supervisors certainly put in many hours. They still have a life outside the organization.

The faster you understand your work supervisor, the better you will be able to work with them and help them to accomplish their goals more effectively.

Expectations
Life oftentimes is about managing expectations. High expectations, which aren't met, lead to disappointment and disillusionment. When we lower our expectations, and they are exceeded, pleasant surprises come our way.

You should not expect your supervisor to cover up mistakes you make, nor should they coddle you. What should you expect from your supervisor? The basics include:

- Written Work Description
    If responsibilities are written down in a clear way, there

will be less likelihood of misunderstanding and confusion.

- Resources

    Providing the tools required for you to complete assigned projects. This can include everything from a workspace, with appropriate equipment, to supplies, and contacts with individuals who can help.

- Organization Policies

    You need to know what is acceptable behavior.

- Feedback

    If you are doing well, it is helpful to know. If not, the same applies. Ask to meet on a regular basis for feedback on your performance and progress on projects. The meetings may be five minutes each morning, or they may be twenty- minute weekly appointments. Make the most of the time, no matter how much is made available.

- Safety

    You should expect your boss to watch out for you regarding certain individuals within the organization who may seek to overstep their authority where your presence or work comes into play.

- Professional Development

    This would include assigning you to projects, which will utilize and grow your skills, introducing you to individuals who may be good networking contacts, and taking you to workshops, seminars, or other types of professional events, either inside or outside the organization.

Observation

Paying attention to the details of your supervisor's life will help you better appreciate and understand their personality and work style. In his excellent (but out-of-print) book, *The New Professional*, Ed Holton writes about getting to know your boss. The following eight points are adapted from p.142 of his book.

Relationship with Subordinates
How close or distant does your boss like to be? Does your boss like to socialize with subordinates?

The Boss's Agenda
What are the highest priorities for your boss? What are her key objectives? What are her biggest problems or issues? How can you help solve them? On what will your boss's performance be judged? What is her agenda?

Your Performance
What is her definition of excellent performance?   What does your boss expect of you?

Office Politics
Who are her enemies? Her friends? (Don't make friends with her enemies.)   How much power does she have?   Is your boss on the fast track for promotion or a slow mover?

Communication
Does your boss prefer a formal or informal style of communication? How well does she respond to suggestions and input? Does your boss prefer to get information verbally in meetings, or by memos, by phone, or by e-mail? How does your boss handle conflict?

Personal Work Habits
What is your boss's peak time of day? Downtime? What are her particular quirks and idiosyncrasies? (You'll have to adapt.) What are your boss's mood cycles? When does she arrive for work and leave?

General Considerations
What are your boss's strengths and weaknesses? (You should help cover her weaknesses.) What pressures does your boss have

to deal with, and how can you relieve them?

Your Boss's Boss
What kind of relationship does your boss have with her boss? How much freedom does your boss have to run her area? (If not much, then you'll need to pay more attention to your boss's boss.)

Working Well
A key concept to working well with your supervisor is to take all your observations and put yourself in their shoes. Think about life from their perspective. They probably want you to:
- Do the work assigned to you.
- See if you can figure out the answer to questions before you ask them.
- Keep them informed of your activities and progress; don't surprise them.
- Take notes and clarify any instructions by verbally going back over them.
- Speak well of your supervisor, as best you can, to other people within the organization and not join in with others to cut her/him down.
- Find ways to help them look good.
- Look for solutions to their problems.
- Accept criticism and learn from it.
- Go the extra mile, and do more than the required minimum.

Difficult Work Relationship
Maybe you have a tough boss – someone who you have tried to get along with, but it just isn't working. If that is the case, there are some actions you can take.

- Continue to perform your responsibilities in an excellent way. A difficult supervisor does not give you permission to ignore your job.

- Make an appointment with your supervisor and try to clarify specific issues (not generalities). Ask what she specifically would like you to do. Going to the person directly is the first and most important step.
- Talk with co-workers to find out how they have successfully worked with their supervisor. Take notes. Test their advice.
- If you have hooked up with a coach or mentor, objectively go over your situation with them and seek advice.
- Inform your campus internship advisor of the situation.
- If you have been advised to do so by more than one person, cautiously go to your supervisor's boss. This should be done only as a last resort.

Remember, there are some people in this world with whom you will never become friends and will never work well together. That is part of life. Do your best to fulfill your responsibilities, but keep your eyes open for ways to tactfully move away from such a relationship.

VARIETY IS THE SPICE OF LIFE

Nature provides us with a world of tremendous variety. Each part plays its role, and many contribute directly to our enjoyment and well-being. Here are just a few facts to consider:

- There are approximately 750 types of trees in North America and over 100,000 worldwide.
- Over 260,000 species of flowers can be found around the globe.
- At least 10,500 types of birds inhabit our planet.
- No small number of fish species swim in the waters of the earth. The most recent count is close to 30,000.
- The animal kingdom boasts over 1,250,000 identified species.

Think how boring it would be to have just one or two types in each category! What if, for example, there was only one type of bird, or fish, or flower? With each of these there is variation in color, size, shape and other unique attributes. Consider further that none of these live and function in isolation from other aspects of the created order. There is a marvelous interchange between them.

Trees are relaxing to look at and they seem to just stand there not doing anything significant. Are you aware, however, that even though you can't see the process occurring, they give off life-sustaining oxygen? Did you know one willow tree can process fifteen gallons of waste per day including dioxin, ammonia, solvents, oil and gas, PCBs and more? Did you know a tree recently discovered in Bolivia yields an antibiotic that kills drug-resistant staph, e. coli, and salmonella, but is gentle enough to be used as a mouthwash? Trees make a tremendous contribution to our world, but you would never know it from just looking at them.

Just as we enjoy variety throughout nature, so we should enjoy variety in the people we meet and with whom we work. There is variation in size, shape, color, age, background, language, gender, religious belief, personality type, and abilities/disabilities. Each one can make unique contributions to the workplace. Research has shown that when problems are addressed by people who have different personality types and training, a much more robust answer, or set of solutions, is developed.

Just because someone is different from you doesn't mean they don't have something positive to offer. Encourage them by highlighting the positive qualities you observe in them. As you do with nature, take time to appreciate your co-workers.

TEAMWORK

You may feel as if you work best on your own. It may be true that you are very productive and creative in a somewhat isolated environment. But today's organizations place a high priority on individuals being able to work well within a team.

Teams can be difficult. Human beings seek to associate with people like themselves. The most effective teams, however, are composed of people who have different personality types, different majors or jobs, and different outside interests. When teams are composed of diverse people, rich thinking occurs and specific perspectives are challenged. Of course, there is always the danger that not everyone will pull their weight with a project. When that happens, problems can ensue.

For a team effort to be successful, certain actions must be carried out and guidelines set in place. These include:

- Clear, unambiguous objective(s) for the team as a whole
- Clear, unambiguous responsibilities for each member
- Team leader is appointed or voted in by the team
- Clear, unambiguous, regular communication between members – including ongoing feedback on each person's responsibilities
- Resources to accomplish assigned tasks are readily available
- Timeline is developed and understood by all

A well-worn proverb says, "Failing to plan is planning to fail."

Before a team starts to actually move forward on their objective, the above items need to be worked out and settled in everyone's mind. Taking time to address these items, and making sure all people and components are integrated from the very start, will save time and headaches later.

EMAIL ETIQUETTE

Common courtesy is a subject dealt with elsewhere in this book, but it is something that is applicable to the use of email. Remember that the person on the other end cannot see your face or your gestures to better "read" you, so your email must communicate your thoughts and feelings accurately.

While the guidelines below are not comprehensive, they will provide you with a starting point for email etiquette. Please keep in mind that it is best to err on the side of being too formal and professional than not professional enough.

Do not send anything that you would not be comfortable seeing in tomorrow's headlines. Email is more like a postcard than a sealed envelope with a letter in it.

- Treat email like any other business communication; watch your spelling and grammar.
- It is best to use the Blind Carbon Copy (BCC) feature when sending an email message to a large number of people. When you place email addresses in the BCC: field of a message, those addresses are invisible to the recipients of the email.
- Read what you have written before you send it.
- Be succinct, yet tactful.
- Break up the text by using short lines and paragraphs; this

makes it easier for the recipient to read.

- Be sure to fill in the "Subject" line with concise and informative language; this allows the recipient to file, prioritize, and retrieve it easily. It is considered rude to leave the subject line blank.
- Do not address the recipient with "Hey" or "Yo!"
- Always address professionals using a formal greeting such as "Ms. Chopra," or "Mr. Mason," or "Dr. Tan." Address them by their first name only if they have given you permission to do so.
- Writing in all UPPERCASE and/or **BOLD** letters is considered SHOUTING! at the recipient.
- Copyright laws apply to electronic mail as well as to printed media.
- Use lists and indentations to make your points stand out.
- Do not forward or edit an email without the original sender's consent.
- When replying to a message sent to multiple addressees, only respond to the sender, unless all recipients need to hear from you.
- Try to respond promptly to email messages, even if it is to let the sender know you have received the email and you will reply in full later.
- Refrain from adding too many attachments as it is bulky for the recipient, and they may lack the software necessary to read the attachment.
- Do not send chain emails. These are emails that tell you to forward the information to many other people.
- Remember that all laws that pertain to discrimination, defamation, and harassment (verbal, emotional, and sexual) pertain to electronic communication as well.

On the next page is an example of how to use a subject line well and how to provide all necessary information in the body of the email.

This message has not been sent.

	To...	pmalone@jupiterent.com
Send	Cc...	
	Subject:	Meeting Reminder - Project X - Thursday @ 9:00 am - Vision Room

This is a reminder that a meeting will be held on Thursday at 9:00 am in the Vision Room on the 4th Floor.

Our purpose is to discuss and outline the primary points of Project X. Individual assignments will be made at the meeting.

Be sure to bring the printout of the background document, your initial thoughts on funding sources, and recommendations for support contacts.

If you have any questions, please reply to this email or call me at x4545.

Zachary Winston
Project Management Intern
Room 225 - Main Building
Supervisor: Karin Shuler

PHONE ETIQUETTE

Using the phone well speaks volumes about you as a person. Remember that the person on the other end cannot see your face or your gestures to better "read" you, so your voice must communicate your thoughts and feelings accurately. Following are some guidelines for proper use of the phone.

- Express yourself clearly and concisely.
- If you are the caller, it is helpful to identify yourself as soon as possible - "Hello. This is Brittany Dodge from Omni College, may I please speak with Mr. Samuel Smith?"
- Make sure your conversations with busy people are short and to the point.
- If you call the wrong number, apologize - "I'm sorry. I must have the wrong number. Thank you."
- When giving your name and number, be sure to speak slowly so the receiver can write down the information. Spell your name. Speak your phone number in two or three-digit segments. People process numbers best when given in small chunks.
- Try to avoid placing others on hold.
- Keep the receiver informed. Never put someone on hold for an extended period of time (more than 60 seconds) without going back and saying, "I'm still checking on your problem/ question, would you like to continue holding or would you prefer that I call you back when I find an answer?"
- If you have a call on another line, it is polite to ask the cur-

rent receiver if they mind being put on hold - "Excuse me, may I put you on hold for a few seconds?" When returning to the phone call, be sure to thank the person for waiting.

- Always ask permission before placing someone on speakerphone. If you place a call using the speakerphone, greet the person and immediately say something like the following - "Hello Ms. Summers. I have you on speakerphone. Is that OK?"
- When receiving a call, answer the phone with a simple, "Hello, (insert your first and last name) speaking."
- Never eat while talking on the telephone.
- Listen actively.
- Always return calls within 24 hours.
- Turn off cell phones and set pagers to vibrate when in a meeting, a dinner engagement, at the movies, or any other place where the ringing and conversation would disturb others.

PROFESSIONAL CARD

Professionals often exchange cards as a means of introduction and networking. Even though you are an intern, you should have your own card. You may use them in committee meetings, at community events, association gatherings, luncheons, receptions, business after hours events, workshops, seminars, conferences, and job/internship fairs.

Professional cards should be carried at all times – in your pocket, purse, or wallet. Have them ready to hand out to the new people you meet.

Template resources may be found at Avery.com and Microsoft's website.

Basic information to include on your card is:

- your name
- where you are interning
- your title "Electrical Engineering Intern"
- your email address (be sure it is professional – don't use anything like *hunkamania@yahoo.com* or *prettyinpink@ gmail.com*)
- if permitted by the organization, use their logo
- your LinkedIn profile URL

You may choose to order cards at a local print/copy center or online, but be careful of costs. An inexpensive, higher-quality online source is Vistaprint.com. You should also have an electronic card, or at least some further contact information ready to send along with all email.

NETWORKING

Networking is simply establishing a link with another person. Building a professional network is very important. Though you may not wish to believe it, the old adage is often true – "It's not what you know, but who you know that counts." You need to have a vibrant skill set and a solid educational background. When those are combined with a continuously growing network of professional contacts, you increase your chances of being offered new opportunities.

Networking can be rather informal. You may, for instance, meet someone in a restaurant or at the airport. That person may later turn out to be a link to another internship, a future job, or a source person for new business.

The process can also be systematic and well thought out. Consider some of the following ideas:

- Develop a plan to cultivate informal interpersonal contacts and relationships for three purposes - to compile information on your job search, to gain exposure to the job market, and to gather names and referrals.
- Plan and structure your effort to start with friends, acquaintances, and relatives and then move on to co-workers and supervisors.
- During breaks, lunch, or slow times ask co-workers about their jobs. Find out what they do on a day-to-day basis -

what do they like/dislike.

- Ask how their jobs compare to colleagues in other organizations.
- Get to meet/know the top decision-makers; they can provide valuable insight as to why and how things are done; observe their influence; watch their management style.
- Remember - an effective networking meeting has a predetermined purpose, a structure and an agenda, but it is to be low-pressure, informal and conversational. Do not view it as an interview for a job.
- Take notes! Don't try to keep in your head everything a person talks about. Record their advice. If you don't have anything to write on, record voice notes during the meeting with a digital device, if they have given you prior permission to do so.
- For online, professional networking you need to create an account on LinkedIn.com. This website is the defacto resume' for professionals.

NETWORKING: THE ART OF MINGLING AT EVENTS

Before the Reception/Event

- Think about your purpose for going and what you want to accomplish.
  - Try to secure a participant list prior to the day of the event.
  - Who would you specifically like to meet?
  - What is it that you would like to learn about them or from them?
  - Is there something useful to learn about the organization or facility in which the reception is being held?
  -
- Prepare yourself.
  - Dress appropriately. If it is not stated otherwise on the invitation, dress conservatively in attire that is consistent with your occupation.
  - Don't overdue jewelry or perfume/cologne.
  - Bring along enough business cards. Place them in a convenient pocket for quick access.
  - Read the latest local news. Many potential topics of conversation can be gleaned this way.
  - Research current issues within the particular industry on which the event is focusing.
  - Develop a 15 second "sound bite" introduction of yourself.
  - Take along, and use, breath mints.

Moving Beyond Yourself (Read - *How To Win Friends and Influence People in the Digital Age* by Dale Carnegie Associates)
- Become genuinely interested in other people.
- Smile. It opens doors.
- Remember that a person's name is to that person the sweetest and most important sound in any language. Repeat it back to them several times during the course of the conversation.
- Be a good listener. Encourage others to talk about themselves.
- Talk in terms of the other person's interest.
- Make the other person feel important – and do it sincerely.

Meeting and Greeting People
- Remember that many people feel as apprehensive as you about the event.
- Approach someone else who is standing alone. Otherwise, look for those who seem to just be standing together, but not talking a great deal. Look for those whose "circle" is open, allowing you an entrance.
- If people are holding drinks and/or plates of food, do not extend your hand to shake hands.
- Maintain the individual's personal space – approximately an arm's length.
- Use an honest opening line like, "Excuse me, I hope you don't mind my coming up to you like this, but I don't know a single person here. My name is …"
- Use open-ended questions like, "What are you enjoying about the reception (or conference)?"
- Need ideas for conversation topics? Remember FORD – Ask about their Family, Occupation, Recreation, Dreams. You may also ask about organizational affiliation and mutual acquaintances.
- You can also try to quietly ease into a group by standing on the periphery, listening intently to the

conversation and slowly making your way closer to eventually join in.

Eating and Drinking

- It is wise to refrain from alcohol, even at a "Wine and Cheese" event.
- Remember that, for the most part, receptions are not meant to take the place of a regular meal. Food is served in small proportions. The purpose is for socializing more than eating.
- Do not overfill your plate. Remember, this isn't your last meal. Take a few items at a time and go back for more, if necessary.
- Learn to hold your glass and plate with your left hand, so you can shake hands and pass out business cards with your right hand. If your glass has a stem, hold the base of the glass against the plate with your left thumb.

Afterwards

- Send a note of appreciation to the event sponsor. Handwritten notes are best, but an email is better than nothing.
- Send "Nice to meet you" notes to those you met and with whom you exchanged business cards.
- Record your contacts, titles, phone numbers, email addresses, etc…in a central place. You may do this with a smartphone app, database, spreadsheet, journal, or notebook.

Last, but not least, HAVE FUN!

 ## COMMUNICATION - ORAL

Year after year surveys of employers indicate excellent oral and written communication skills are at the top of every recruiter's checklist for potential employees. A person who speaks well in one-on-one conversations and to groups, small or large, will set themselves apart from the majority. Being able to speak cogently using a rich vocabulary is a skill that can, and should, be developed.

One-On-One
People normally enjoy talking about themselves. If you want to open the door to a good one-on-one conversation with a person you have just met, ask the other person questions about what they do related to work and what interests they have outside work. Open questions are intended to engage a person in dialogue. Examples would be "What do you think about...?" or "If you were in charge, what would you do differently?" or "How do you successfully reduce stress with all your challenges?"

Good preparation... is crucial to success

Sincere questions are a great conversation starter. Be sure to read *How To Win Friends and Influence People in the Digital Age* by Dale Carnegie Associates .

Speeches – Preparation
Good preparation, whether you are speaking to a small group committee meeting or to a large audience, is crucial to success. You can begin by asking the questions mentioned above. Use a mind map to sketch out your speech – MindMapping.com

- Who is the audience?
- Why are they gathered?
- What do they want you to present or need to hear?
- When will the speech take place?
  - If it is after lunch for instance, you may have some sleepy people with the "I would like a nap" look.
- Where is the speech taking place?
  - Does the room have AV capability, if you need it? What type of atmosphere does it project (dark and dreary, or bright and upbeat)?

Your speech should be in a logical sequence with at least three basic components:

- Introduction – presentation of your main topic and what the speech will cover
- Body – supporting arguments, illustrations, up-to-date accurate data
- Conclusion – re-state your primary point (thesis), describe the action steps you feel need to be taken, and thank them

Often it is helpful to include a story. Telling a story is like opening a window. It allows a fresh breeze of enlightenment to enter the mind of the hearer. Stories allow plain facts to be placed in a more colorful context, which leads to better understanding and retention. To learn more, ask your favorite search engine for "Storytelling Tips".

Practice makes perfect, so be sure to review your speech several times. Stand up, use your index cards, outline, or PowerPoint and act it out just as if you were actually presenting. You may want to video record yourself, so you can see and hear everything from an "outsider's" perspective. If you make a mistake, just correct it and move on. You don't need to apologize profusely. Skype or FaceTime a friend and have them evaluate you in real time.

Speeches – Presentation
Body Language
- Stand up straight
- Use appropriate hand gestures
  - They should fit your comment
    - "We have a wide range of possibilities" – arms in front of you and move them outward from the center of your body
    - "This is very important" – one hand pointing or moving slightly downward with a sudden stop
- Make good eye contact with your audience throughout the presentation
  - People will get the distinct sense you are speaking directly to them

Voice
- Volume - speak loud enough so the person furthest from you can hear easily; don't mumble
- Clarity - enunciate your words
- Speed – practice pacing yourself; do not rush it
- Tone – vary your inflection; do not speak in a boring, monotone voice

Movement
- Do not feel tied to the podium, if you are behind one

Appearance
- Dress appropriately for the occasion, and remember those

higher up in the department or organization may stop in to hear what you have to say.

Audio-Visuals
- Be sure to check equipment and materials ahead of time to make sure everything is working.
- PowerPoint or website like Prezi.com
  ○ Beware of too many words on a slide or screen view
  ○ Use a picture or graphic with no words or just a few
- Document cameras
  ○ Allows you to place sheets of paper, magazines, and books on them for display on a screen. Caution: Do not move items around. Even slight movements seem exaggerated to the audience and will diminish the effectiveness of your presentation.
- Flip Charts
- Post-It Pads to hang removable sheets from walls and boards
- White Boards
- Handouts
  ○ Tell your audience ahead of time if you have prepared an outline or other notes, so that they don't need to take notes unnecessarily

Allow time for questions. Your audience may need to clarify an issue or point you made.

End your presentation with a few minutes to spare. An early ending is appreciated by an audience.

COMMUNICATION - WRITTEN

Writing, without doubt, has been a major part of your education thus far. Research papers, stories of fiction and non-fiction, book reports, and many other methods have been employed to help you develop good writing skills.

Two problems employers consistently identify with interns and recent graduates are grammar and wordiness. In recent years, rules of proper grammar have not been emphasized by various segments of society, including the publishing industry. But employers need those skilled in grammar to craft coherent internal and external messages. Notice in the following two sentences what a simple comma can do. "Let's eat Grandma" and "Let's eat, Grandma." The first example means Grandma is going to be eaten by her grandchildren. In the second example, the grandchildren are imploring Grandma to serve food to them. A comma saved Grandma's life! Take advantage of tools like *grammarbook.com* .

The second problem employers encounter is students who continue to write lengthy reports, as if they are still in school writing a ten or twenty-page paper for a course. Maybe you have felt pressure in school as you reach the halfway point in a writing project and realize you don't have enough material to legitimately fill the rest of the paper. What's the solution? If you are like many students, you fill it in with meaningless fluff. Now you find yourself in an internship and you carry over your learned behavior of lengthy writing into the professional environment. Stop! Don't do it!

Learn to write well. A wise editor of a magazine once said, "We look for efficiency of language." Many sentences can contain fewer words and still get the point across with impact. "Vigorous writing is concise. A sentence should contain no unnecessary words, a paragraph no unnecessary sentences, for the same reason a drawing should have no unnecessary lines and a machine no unnecessary parts."

– p.23, *The Elements of Style* by Strunk & White

Executive Summary
Most organizations – business, non-profit, and government - are not usually looking for lengthy treatises on a given subject. They are more interested in writing that is succinct, as you find in an executive summary, which is often only one to three pages in length. As you may have noticed, the subjects covered in this book are written in an executive summary type of format – short and to the point. People have written books on these subjects, so the purpose here is to provide only the most salient points.

A few ideas you should consider:

- As mentioned in the section on Oral Communication, Who, What, When, Where, Why, and How are the words with which key questions begin. These are the six sides of a multi-faceted approach to better understanding a situation. Ask these questions as you draft your written piece. For example, who is your audience?
- Spell check – always on and always used.
- Grammar check should be used as well.
- Diversify word usage by using the thesaurus included with word processing software.
- Track changes. When creating a document, which will have

multiple revisions, made by you and/or others, be sure to use the "track changes" feature. You can usually find it in the "tools" menu at the top of the screen.

- An executive summary is a standalone document most often used to summarize main points and to make a recommendation. Background facts, experience, and/or research form the basis for the construction of it.

Sometimes more than one document is used in its preparation. Accuracy is very important, since the readers will not always have access to the background material. Some components to consider including are:

- Issue or problem stated in a few sentences
- Brief history or timeline of events
- Analysis of the issue
- Alternate solutions with pros and cons
- Clear recommendation(s) with justification, based on analysis and input from concerned parties

If you need to write an executive summary of your internship or co-op experience for your school and/or your organization, consider the following to prepare a two-page report, which summarizes your internship experience. It should include:

- Information about the organization
- Responsibilities and expectations
- Work accomplished and projects participated in
- New skills or understandings you acquired
- Future plans and how they have been influenced by the internship
- How well you were prepared by, and recommendations you may have for, your academic department, in order to better prepare future students for an internship like yours

Consider the following abbreviated sample, including sub-headings.

EXECUTIVE SUMMARY
FALL INTERNSHIP – DANA SCULLEY
FAMILY STUDIES

Introduction
I interned at Great Springs Health Systems as a Child Life Assistant. Great Springs employs over 1,000 employees in four locations within the greater metro area. My supervisor was Ms. M. Theresa.

I developed four learning objectives, along with appropriate resources for accomplishing them and several means to verify my completion of them. The objectives were to learn how children deal with the stress of pre and post-surgery, to research...

Work/Projects
Most of the work I completed revolved around three major projects – development of an interactive stress-reduction program for children awaiting surgery, a class for parents...

Learning
I began this internship with more than a little trepidation, but as I approach the end of my twelve weeks, my self-confidence has grown tremendously. Several new skills and abilities have been acquired over this time. Not only did I learn how to develop effective programs, but I also learned that children...

Future Plans
As a result of this internship, I have decided to attend graduate school for a Master's degree, in preparation for the Child Life profession. To better my chances of being accepted into graduate school, I'm planning on working this next year with a hospital or other related agency...

Preparation/Recommendations
My studies have proven to be very useful to me. I was able to see and

better understand a number of issues discussed in classes. Of particular use were portions of Dynamics of Family Interaction, especially the module on...

If I could make a recommendation to my academic department, it would be...

Meeting Notes
You may be asked to take notes at committee meetings. Be sure to inform your supervisor that you will be including only the highlights of the meeting, not a word for word commentary on it. Ask if she/he has any problems with that format. A clear, simple design to use is the following:

- Date
- Time
- Place
- Purpose
- Attendees
- Discussion Highlights and Key Thoughts
  - Example
    - Project research – concern over lack of customer qualitative input
    - Staffing – qualitative study calls for temporary addition to team
- Decisions Made
  - Example
    - Action – Rebecca will immediately re-assign a staff person to the team for a period of four weeks, with a re-evaluation of progress after three weeks.
- Responsibilities Distributed
- Next Meeting Date/ Time/Place

Taking/Leaving Messages

Some organizations still have individuals take written messages. Whether you need to write it, email a message, or pass it along in some other format, be sure to gather the information (or provide it, if you are leaving a message) shown below. If leaving a voicemail, remember to speak slowly, enunciate your words, and repeat the key information such as your name, phone, and/or email.

- Date
- Time
- From
  - Ask for the caller's full name and title
- Organization
  - What organization does the caller represent?
- Phone Number
  - At what numbers can the caller be reached? If possible, try to obtain their cell number.
- Message
- Follow-Up
  - Will the caller try to reach the person again? If so, what day and time? Or...where and when can they be reached?
  - When a name is provided, repeat it. Ask the caller to spell their name, if you can't quite grasp the pronunciation.
  - Phone numbers should be repeated and spoken in groups of three or less – e.g., 215...722...39...76. The brain is geared to hear numbers more easily in small chunks.

VIRTUAL MEETINGS

Virtual meetings are gaining importance as a cost-effective way to conduct business. They save on transportation, lodging, and meal costs. Virtual meetings come in a variety of forms - webinars, videoconferencing, collaborating by way of programs like Skype, instant messaging, or sharing files through a collaborative software program and server.

Whether the meetings are one-to-one through a mobile device or group-to-group through a sophisticated meeting program, they offer the opportunity for you to present yourself well. Keep in mind the fact that these are still meetings, no matter the means by which they are conducted.

Some items to which you should pay close attention are listed below. Many of these apply to face-to-face meetings as well.

- Appearance
  Dress appropriately for your normal work environment. If you are participating in the meeting from your home, be sure to dress and groom yourself just as if you were in your work environment.
- Conduct
  Be careful what you do, because everyone else will see. Watch your posture; don't slouch. If you need to blow your nose, leave the room. If you have a persistent cough, excuse yourself from the meeting and leave the room (or mute the sound from your end). Do not eat

during the meeting. Doing so doesn't leave a good impression and may result in unnecessary and irritating sounds. You also don't want to be caught trying to speak with food in your mouth.

- Background
  If possible, choose a background that does not have distracting designs or colors. You want people to pay attention to you, not what is behind you.

- Software Programs
  If your meeting is being conducted through a PC, close and quit all software programs not needed for the meeting. You don't want an instant message, for instance, to pop-up that may be seen by others in your virtual session.

- Sound
  It is best to mute your end of the call until you have something to say. This helps overall clarity of the sound and keeps unwanted sounds from intruding. Beyond that, turn off music, put cell phones on vibrate, forward your landline so it doesn't ring in your work space. In other words, keep your end of the meeting quiet. If you are in an open environment where people are normally talking, do your best to muffle the sound or ask your co-workers to keep their voices down during the meeting.

- Paperwork
  Prior to the meeting, assemble all the papers you may need (reports, minutes, spreadsheets, etc.). Open any necessary documents which may be on your computer. You want to be prepared. Once the meeting has begun, you don't want to be fumbling around looking for items while others wait.

- Notetaking
  Be sure to have a pen, pencil, and paper readily available. Don't rely on your memory. Check out the video

- "Meeting Notes Made Easy" on **InternQube.com** for some helpful insights. If you would like to record the conversation, you must ask the other participants if that is OK with them.
- Practice

  Check out the software and procedures ahead of time. Make sure the camera angle and sound quality are just right. Sometimes you will need to download a separate piece of software for the meeting software to function correctly. Do it the day before and test it to make sure it works. You also want to make sure you understand the sign-on procedure.

Remember – virtual meetings are conducted with real people dealing with real issues, which have real world consequences. Use these meetings to present yourself and your ideas in the best light possible.

 ***ETHICAL BEHAVIOR***

The subject of ethics can be very "heady" and philosophical. It covers a broad spectrum of activity. There are ethical guidelines for a host of careers – medicine, law, business, counseling, etc., so there is no way to cover the specifics of it for every career choice.

Ethical behavior, simply stated, is rooted in the belief that there are proper and improper, good and bad, right and wrong, ways to act in a given situation.   For instance, cultures around the world would generally agree that you should not take what doesn't belong to you.   Examples would be printing personal items on the business photocopier without paying for them, plagiarizing ideas and words, taking time away from your job to conduct personal business (without permission of your employer), and so much more.   Another generally agreed upon principle is to speak the truth.   Do not lie about a person or event, whether you are under oath in a courtroom or not.

Do to others as you would have them do to you.

If you do not know how to behave ethically in your chosen profession, check out the website of your professional association. Most have a statement of professional or ethical behavior.   If you follow a particular religious belief, no doubt it has a set of principles or standards by which you are to conduct your life, so it would be another good source.

An excellent book is Life Principles by Dr. Bruce Weinstein – TheEthicsGuy.com. His website has many useful resources – *www. theethicsguy.com*. Dr. Weinstein wrote a column for *BusinessWeek.com* addressing college graduates. He has some sage advice for you.

Congratulations! Your hard work and persistence have paid off, and you are now on your way to a successful career in business.

In the coming months you'll be getting a lot of advice from family, friends, and general well-wishers, but please allow me, an ethicist, to offer mine as well. After all, many of the biggest crises today are a result of unethical conduct in business, and in the most recent annual Gallup Ethics and Honesty poll, business executives, advertising practitioners, and stockbrokers were among the least-trusted professionals. By taking the following guidelines to heart, you'll let the world know that you are a person of honor and integrity and are someone clients and colleagues can trust.

1. LISTEN TO THE WHISPERS

Frances Hesselbein, Chairman of the Board of Governors of the Leader to Leader Institute (formerly the Peter F. Drucker Foundation for Nonprofit Management) and former CEO of the Girl Scouts of the USA, speaks of the importance of "listening to the whispers" you hear every time you're about to make a decision. She is referring not to the rumor mill but to the voice within that keeps you on the right track.

No matter what station you occupy within an organization—unpaid intern, midlevel executive, or president—you will be tempted to take the low road from time to time. Perhaps a client will ask you for a favor that goes against company policy.

Maybe your boss will tell you to do something that is ethically or legally questionable. Possibly you'll be torn between covering up a mistake you've made or owning up to it. You can talk yourself into just about any decision, but if you follow Hesselbein's wise counsel, you'll make the best decision.

2. KEEP YOUR PROMISES

It seems quaint, perhaps even naive, to talk about the importance of being true to your word, but trustworthiness isn't a nicety of doing business; it's a necessity. Clients are more likely to continue giving you their business and to recommend you when they know you mean what you say. Your company is more likely to keep you on board, to promote you, and to give you a raise when you consistently do what you say you will. You earn the respect of your colleagues when you honor the promises you make.

The contract you sign with the organization is a legal document, but at its most fundamental level it is a covenant, a form of promise-making. You promise to fulfill the responsibilities in your job description, and your employer promises to pay you, to provide a safe working environment and, one hopes, to provide health-care benefits, a retirement plan, and a generous amount of paid vacation.

As with any promise, if either party reneges, the pact is broken. You can't be expected to keep working if your employer stops paying you. Likewise, good employees know that being true to their word means taking the job description seriously, day in and day out. You trust your friends to keep their word, and you justifiably end friendships when this is no longer the case. Don't your clients, colleagues, and boss deserve the same level of commitment from you that you ask of your friends?

3. SPEAK UP

At some point—probably more than once—in your career, you will encounter someone at work doing something he or she shouldn't be doing. When this happens, it will be very tempting to ignore it. Don't. If you discover shady goings-on at your company, you not only have a right to speak up, you have an ethical obligation to do so. "All that is necessary for the triumph of evil is that good [people] do nothing," Edmund Burke said. No one likes confrontations, but the simple act of observing wrongdoing sometimes calls upon you to do or say something, even though it would be simpler to keep quiet. If Sherron Watkins, Cynthia Cooper, and Coleen Rowley hadn't taken action where they worked, the scandals at Enron, WorldCom, and the FBI might never have been exposed.

4. BE A FORCE FOR GOOD

Google's corporate motto, "Don't be evil," speaks to an ethical principle that applies to all of us: Do No Harm. But "don't be evil" doesn't go far enough. The real objective is to be a force for good. Applying your considerable knowledge and skills toward the service of others is what business—and life in general— ought to be about.

Imagine that you're on your deathbed, reviewing how you spent your life. If the most you can say is, "All right, maybe I was a bit selfish, but at least I never hurt anyone," would you feel you realized your potential as a human being?

5. USE THE YOUTUBE TEST

"Don't do anything you wouldn't want to see in a newspaper headline." So went the old-school advice for making the right choices. It's time for an update: "Avoid saying or doing anything you wouldn't want to have posted on YouTube, Facebook, or MySpace." Anything you say or do within the vicinity of a cell phone, Flip, or BlackBerry can become part of the public record, so it behooves you to act and speak cautiously, whether you're on or off the job.

The above guidelines are based on the five fundamental principles of ethics: Do No Harm, Respect Others, Be Fair, and Be Loving. They provide a solid foundation for making the best decisions possible not just at work but at home, in your community, and everywhere else.

May you find much success in the next phase of your life, and may that success come from your commitment to having the highest standards in all that you do.

Following the Golden Rule, varying versions of which are found in several of the world's religions, may serve as a guide for you. It states, "Do to others as you would have them do to you." - Luke 6:31, *The Holy Bible*

 ***INTUITION***

"The intuitive mind is a sacred gift and the rational mind is a faithful servant. We have created a society that honors the servant and has forgotten the gift." – Albert Einstein

Most of our lives are spent using our rational minds for day-to-day activities. Our minds gather information, remember, organize, categorize, problem solve, and perform a host of operations necessary for our healthy functioning at home, work, and during recreation. But life does not consist of only what we can see with our physical eyes. There are times when we experience something beyond our rational minds, which we may call intuition.

People refer to intuition in a variety of ways – as an impression, a hunch, gut feeling, or instinct. It is something most people encounter at one point or another. The feelings we have may relate to our immediate circumstance, or they may somehow be connected to a future event. Though intuition sounds ethereal, it is an ability, which can be developed and applied to everyday situations. It is a tool for your professional toolbox.

As you observe and participate in many different experiences at your current internship, and through multiple internships, you build a reservoir of data and connections, which your conscious and sub-conscious mind can then use to better direct you in future circumstances.

Some individuals and groups would take intuition a step further. One of these is the Institute of HeartMath. "Intuition is the process of perceiving or knowing things to a high degree of certainty without conscious reasoning: knowledge of events such as an act of nature that has yet to happen; or knowledge of a distant material object such as an as-yet unseen obstruction blocking the highway ahead."

The Institute's researchers have conducted controlled and scientifically validated studies, which have led them to expand the definition of intuition to include "not only conscious perception by the mind alone, but also by the body's entire psycho-physiological system. This perception often is evidenced by a range of emotions and measurable physiological changes exhibited or detected throughout the body…"

The above quote is taken from their excellent webpage dealing with this topic. The Institute of HeartMath provides a very simple technique called Quick Coherence to aid relief of stress and help you to be more intuitive. I recommend this technique and the organization to help you be more intuitive – HeartMath.org/resources/heartmath-tools.

As you go about your daily routine, listen to your intuition. You may save yourself from greater stress, anxiety, and trouble.

 *CREATIVITY*

"What a good artist understands is that nothing comes from nowhere. All creative work builds on what came before. Nothing is completely original." – Austin Kleon, *Steal Like An Artist*

Being creative is seeing the same thing as everybody else but thinking of ways to use it differently, or how parts of it may be adapted for a whole new process or product. Apple's fabled iPod began as a collection of parts that already existed in different products – screen, hard drive, and buttons. They were reconfigured, made smaller, and driven by software code. The iPhone built off this concept and added telephonic capability. This is simplifying Apple's achievements, of course, but this is basically what they did. Other individuals and organizations do the same.

Creativity is not a mystery. You have the ability to be creative; however, a few factors influence you. Motivation plays a key role, as does the environment you are in, and the belief that you can be creative. Yes, believing you are creative actually helps you to be more creative.

Obstacles to Creativity
- Being too busy and/or getting too involved with a problem
- Having conflicting goals and objectives
- Not allowing enough time for you to relax
- Fearing criticism

- Lacking confidence
- Stressing – the over-taxed state of your mind and body
- Believing you aren't creative
- Working in a "sterile" environment
- Feeling the demand for quick results
- Being hemmed in by rigid rules, barriers and routines

Increasing Your Creativity
- Give yourself permission to be creative
  - No idea, or set of ideas, is dumb
- Remove personal blocks to creativity
  - For instance, try not to be embarrassed by your own ideas, or be aware that things can be done differently.
- Gain firsthand experience
  A Chinese proverb states:
  I hear: I forget
  I see: I remember
  I do: I understand
- Travel
  - Broadens and refreshes your outlook, and it exposes you to new people, customs, ideas and ways of living. Take photos and keep a diary.
- Associate yourself with seemingly creative people
  - Look for people who are fun to talk to and have a keen sense of interest in life.
- Work with children
  - A child's world is filled with fantasy. Make the effort to interact and learn from them. Try the association game – "What does that look like to you?"
- Play games
  - Pictionary, charades, Scrabble, Boggle, chess, checkers, etc.
- Take up a hobby
  - Drawing, painting, sculpture, orienteering, or ham radio.

- Read
  - On a topic of interest from various viewpoints
  - About things you don't know about or understand
  - Biographies can be helpful.
  - Magazines can provide good stimuli in a short amount of time. Read a certain type of magazine and then write a story or two in that style.
  - Try your hand at drawing some cartoons to illustrate what is found in it.
- Write
  - It forces you to utilize many phases of the creative process.
- Exercise
  - Increases the flow of blood to the brain and helps re lieve stress.
- Develop some personal rituals
  - One writer would play Spanish flamenco music before beginning to write. Mort Walker, the cartoonist who drew Beetle Bailey, would soak one foot in hot water and the other in cold water. John Steinbeck wrote letters to his publisher in a notebook as a warm-up to writing "East of Eden".
- Listen to music
  - Avoid music with lyrics, sudden changes in volume, or music that demands your attention. Brahms, Chopin, Beethoven and Vivaldi are recommended.
- Relax
  - Some people like to soak in a bathtub or take a long shower to open their creative sense.
  - Enjoy a massage.

Resources for Consideration
- Austin Kleon
  - Book - *Steal Like An Artist*
  - *www.austinkleon.com*

- Roger von Oech
  - Book – *A Whack on the Side of the Head*
  - Book – *Expect the Unexpected*
  - *http://blog.creativethink.com/*
- IDEO
  - *http://www.ideo.com/*
  - *https://www.ideo.org/*
  - *http://www.openideo.com/*
  - *http://99u.com/articles/7001/10-Awesome-Videos-On-Idea-Execution-The-Creative-Process*

 **DEEP WORK**

Stop for a moment. What sounds vie for your attention? A ping indicating a new message on WhatsApp? A chime from a new iMessage? The sound of an incoming video call? A ding indicating new email (in multiple email accounts you may have)? What other "voices" call you? Instagram? Facebook? Binge watching a Netflix series? Friends urging you to abandon your work to indulge in some fun, but time-wasting activity?

Our lives grow more distracted every day. We find it more and more difficult to spend time focused on a single task without any interruptions. It is doing us, and our world, harm. Your employer needs focused work from its employees. Our world needs solutions to many pressing problems. One distinct means of meeting those needs is deep work.

"Deep work is the ability to focus without distraction on a cognitively demanding task. It's a skill that allows you to quickly master complicated information and produce better results in less time. Deep work will make you better at what you do and provide the sense of true fulfillment that comes from craftsmanship. In short, deep work is like a super power in our increasingly competitive twenty-first century economy. And yet, most people have lost the ability to go deep—spending their days instead in a frantic blur of e-mail and social media, not even realizing there's a better way." – calnewport.com/books/deep-work

Carl Jung, the famous Swiss psychiatrist, retreated often to Bollingen Tower to think and write without distraction. As a result, he went on to influence the world through his writings. Cal Newport points out, "Indeed, if you study the lives of other influential figures from both distant and recent history, you'll find that a commitment to deep work is a common theme." Stories are told, for instance, about J.K. Rowling's abandonment of all social media and distractions during the writing of her famous Harry Potter novels.

Bill Gates, co-founder of Microsoft Corporation and one of the richest men in the world, spent eight weeks removed from all distractions to write Altair Basic, the foundational code for the first personal computer. He was a student at Harvard, but "Gates ignored the exam cramming he was supposed to be doing and even stopped playing poker. For eight weeks, he, Allen, and Davidoff holed up day and night at the Aiken lab making history…In the wee hours of the morning, Gates would sometimes fall asleep at the terminal. 'He'd be in the middle of a line of code when he'd gradually tilt forward until his nose touched the keyboard,' Allen said. 'After dozing an hour or two, he'd open his eyes, squint at the screen, blink twice, and resume precisely where he'd left off — a prodigious feat of concentration.' " – Dawn of a Revolution by Walter Isaacson, Harvard Gazette

Whether you realize it or not, you have an urgent need to engage in deep work. You, and those around you, will benefit. Here are a few initial steps to get you started:

- Turn off all your digital devices. This will be extremely hard, because you, like millions of others, are addicted to them.
- Take a note pad, pen, or pencil and retreat to someplace without any, or very few, distractions – a library, museum, park, or some other secluded place. The genius of Leonardo da Vinci was nurtured in this same way by his university professor. He was told to leave the classroom and go out to observe nature. His observations were recorded in words

and drawings in a journal. Leonardo continued this practice throughout his life and went on to become one of the world's greatest thinkers and inventors.

- Learn to see without your eyes being glued to any screen.
- Learn to hear with nothing in, or covering, your ears.
- Learn to write by hand without a keyboard.
- Learn to think without constant interruptions.

An excellent resource is Cal Newport's book, *Deep Work: Rules for Focused Success in a Distracted World*. Check out the video summary at InternQube.com. He has other resources for students. Learn more at calnewport.com

SYSTEMS THINKING

Systems are made up of interdependent and interrelated parts. They have purpose, and all the parts have to be present and functioning in their place for optimum performance. For example, a car is made up of many individual parts, but together they function as a system. The key or start button interacts with the computer and electrical system to ignite the gas and force the pistons to generate power, so that when the transmission is put into Drive, the driveshaft begins turning and the wheels start to move. Electric cars, of course, forego an engine entirely and send power from the battery directly to the wheels, but they still function as a system. Similarly, the transportation you take and the control components behind it (traffic lights, subway monitoring, air traffic control) all work to make sure you get from one location to another safely and efficiently.

Nature is a system with many intersecting components. A very simple illustration is the hydrologic, or water, cycle. First, the sun's warmth causes water in streams, lakes, and oceans to vaporize and rise into the air. Water droplets adhere to each other and form into clouds. Second, the water cools down and condenses into liquid water. The third stage is when that cooled water falls back to earth in the form of rain, snow, or sleet. Fourth, the water then collects in the streams, lakes and oceans again, only to begin the cycle all over again. Talk about sustainability! This system is the greatest recycling system ever. Some of the rain that falls on you today may have fallen on the earth a few thousand years ago. The point is systems are everywhere, but we fail to recognize them.

Our tendency is to view people, organizations, processes and decisions as separate from the contexts in which they find themselves. Think about your own life. What contexts, or systems, help shape who you are, what you do, and how you respond to situations? Family, friends, schools, clubs you are a member of, sports teams you belong to, your faith community, co-workers, and so many more elements become an interlocking web of influences. They are sub-systems within the larger system of your life, and similar sub-systems are part of the lives of your supervisors and co-workers. Organizations, too, are systems with many sub-systems.

As Daniel Kim writes in Introduction to Systems Thinking, "... understanding how systems work — and how we play a role in them — lets us function more effectively and proactively within them. The more we understand systemic behavior, the more we can anticipate that behavior and work with systems (rather than being controlled by them) to shape the quality of our lives. To be a true systems thinker, you also need to know how systems fit into the larger context of day-to-day life, how they behave, and how to manage them."

To better understand your organization and function more efficiently within it, create some mind maps highlighting systems which impact you. Take a piece of paper, colored pencils (or crayons or Sharpies) and develop one or more of the following:
- Structural maps - that highlight the organization and its subsystems. Where do you fit within the system? What internal and external forces influence the department you work in? How does this help you understand the pressures you and your co-workers face?
- Key Player maps - to show which individuals and/or organizations are the main actors and how they are connected with

each other. Who influences your supervisor? Are there connections between people across two or more departments? Does this reveal why certain issues remain a problem? Or why projects go more smoothly? Who wields the real power? It may be outside of the managerial hierarchy.

- Issue maps - which lay out the political, social, or economic issues affecting a given constituency or geographic region. Your organization may have a heavy influence in a certain geographic area. Why is that? Does the population of that area fit into a specific socio-economic stratum?

As you approach your professional life, the people you work and associate with, the organizations in which you find yourself, and the problems that you confront, remember to embrace systems thinking. Observe and reflect on how they interact with other people and processes, and why they may interact in that way. By doing this, you will develop some of the top skills employers want, which were mentioned in a previous chapter. As well, you will better understand and manage your web of systems with uncommon insight.

Learn more by watching the video "Systems Thinking – An Introduction" at InternQube.com.

THE VALUE OF CHECKLISTS

As noted elsewhere in this book, writing is important. Taking handwritten notes at meetings, hand-drawing mind maps to understand systems and the forces acting upon them, and re-writing in your own words what you understand from a document or book you are reading are all worthwhile for remembering and analyzing relationships. One other act of writing which can have a huge potential impact on your work is the simple checklist.

Atul Gawande is a surgeon and best-selling author of several books, including *The Checklist Manifesto: How To Get Things Done Right.* He highlights how checklists are used by airline pilots for pre-flight procedures and emergency responses, by hospitals for complex procedures such as surgeries, and by the construction industry.

The construction of large structures takes a planned, coordinated process of ordering materials, scheduling personnel, and many other tasks to make sure the building process proceeds in an efficient manner and is completed by the promised date. Ideally it will also be under budget. A project executive is the one who oversees the whole process from start to finish. To make sure that everything is done in an orderly manner and nothing is missed, this person uses multiple large checklists which have been checked and re-checked by all the contracting groups that will be part of the project. These lists cover the walls of the project executive's primary work area. Gawande writes of his experience at the construction site of a thirty-two story building in Boston, "As I peered in close, I saw a line-by-line, day-by-day listing of every building task that needs to be accomplished, in what order, and when…" He was amazed at the complexity and detail involved. In the end, the checklists served their purpose: the building was completed safely and on time.

Checklists are similar to, but different from, "to-do" lists. They help you to remember and clearly set out the minimum steps necessary in a process. Good checklists are explicit: they specifically address the core of what is required. They help people to remember how to manage a complex problem, clarify priorities, and function better as a team – but they cannot be enforced, except to the extent the team agrees to make them a priority.

So how does this apply to you? Consider critical processes at your work site. Have you observed that some tasks are missed, causing delays, loss of time, and possibly loss of money? If so, a checklist may be just what is needed. No process is too small or too big to be considered.

Here are a few guidelines for creating good checklists:
- Length counts. There should be no more than ten items on any one checklist, depending on the context or situation; otherwise, people tend to begin working around them, or ignoring them.
- Focus on steps that are the most dangerous to skip and most often overlooked.
- Balancing the tension between being too brief and communicating enough to be effective is the most difficult part.
- Use simple and exact wording, and use language or acronyms which are familiar to the profession you are in.
- Appearance matters. Ideally, the checklist in most cases is no more than one page in length, free from clutter, and uses a clean font like Calibri.
- Keep them up-to-date. Even simple ones require frequent

review and ongoing refinement.

Learn more by watching the video on checklists at InternQube. com.

As mentioned before, to-do lists are different than checklists. The best way to manage to-do lists is with your calendar, so you can keep track of what needs done by a certain day and time. Projects can be broken into manageable pieces with your calendar, especially setting aside time for yourself to do deep work. Otherwise, you can use tools like:

- Asana
- Todoist
- Any.do
- Remember the Milk
- Workflowy
- Google Keep

WHAT TO DO WHEN YOU MAKE MISTAKES

Leonardo da Vinci (1452-1519), the great painter, sculptor, architect, engineer and scientist, believed in a concept called Dimostrazione. According to Michael Gelb, author of *How To Think like Leonardo da Vinci*, it is a commitment to test knowledge through experience, persistence, and a willingness to learn from mistakes. Leonardo had firsthand knowledge of the concept, because he made a few large blunders himself.

Consider the time he sought to automate the kitchen of Ludovico Sforza for a two hundred-guest banquet. He "built a new, more powerful stove and a complex system of mechanical conveyor belts to move plates around the kitchen. He also designed and installed a massive sprinkler system in case of fire." (Gelb, p. 79) The day of the banquet arrived and everything went wrong. The kitchen became too crowded, the conveyor belt failed, a fire broke out, and the sprinkler system worked too well and washed the food away in a flood. But Leonardo was undeterred. He never stopped experimenting and learning.

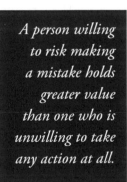

A person willing to risk making a mistake holds greater value than one who is unwilling to take any action at all.

Mistakes come with a hidden surprise – something you need to learn. If you view your mistakes as gifts and learn from them, people will grow to respect you. A person willing to risk making a mistake holds greater value than one who is unwilling to take any action at all. If you read stories of successful individuals, you will find they failed often. But they reflected on what went wrong, picked themselves up, and tried again.

How should you handle mistakes you've made?

- Admit the mistake.
  Don't try to hide it, or hide behind someone or something else. If there is a person(s) directly affected, try to speak with them face to face to express sorrow for what you did.
- Be realistic.
  People are, most likely, going to be upset and may say more than a few choice words to you.
- Maintain perspective.
  It isn't the end of the world. The sun will rise again tomorrow. Ask yourself one question, "Will this matter five years from now?"
- Look for the lesson(s).
  How can you improve as a result of the experience? Once you have identified one or more lessons you've learned, tell your supervisor and, depending on the situation, your co-workers – either face-to-face or by email.
- Talk to someone.
  Call someone who lives or works outside the immediate crisis and ask for a listening ear. Just don't let them convince you to cover over whatever you have done!

COMMON COURTESY

Often we associate common courtesy with saying, "Please," "Thank you," and "Welcome". We use it when we greet people kindly with "Have a good day," and "Please, go before me". It is demonstrated when we hold open a door for someone, turn off our cell phone to have an uninterrupted conversation with an individual, and in numerous other ways.

Unfortunately, "common courtesy" is not what many people exhibit or observe anymore at home, at work, in school, or anywhere else in society. We have grown callous and selfish, and have become rude and uncaring in the process. Our behavior is all about us. We are the center of

Honor one another above yourselves

our own universe and we find ways, consciously and unconsciously, to let other people in on the not-very-well-kept secret of our own importance.

Following are some hints to help you succeed in applying the ancient wisdom of "honor one another above yourselves". They have been adapted/modified from Willipedia, the wiki created by students of Williams College in Williamstown, Massachusetts.

General
  • Say hello to people you meet. If someone else says hello

to you, respond in kind. Bonus points for smiling while saying hello.
- Say "excuse me" rather than just pushing past people in a crowd or a constricted space.
- Wave to, nod, or mouth "thank you" to drivers who stop for you to cross on a pedestrian crossing. It's the law for them to stop, but it's still polite when they do because many don't.
- Look both ways before you cross the street, even if you're at a crosswalk.
- If someone passes gas, make believe you didn't hear it. (Even though you did and it's hilarious.)
- If possible, leave space on the sidewalk so others don't have to walk in water, mud, or snow. If you're walking in a group and one person comes in the opposite direction, move behind someone in your group so the person passing can use the sidewalk as well.
- Be careful how you maneuver with that umbrella; it is easy to accidentally poke someone in the eye.

Conversation
- Don't interrupt someone while they're talking, no matter how insightful you think what you have to say is. This is one of the rudest things one could do in a conversation, though oftentimes people simply aren't aware that they are guilty of doing it. Instead,
  - make sure they've finished speaking and making their point
  - wait a half-second, and then
  - go ahead and say what you wanted to say, and
  - if you miss your chance because someone else chimed in before you, it's OK - life goes on. You're not as interesting as you think, anyway.

Doors
- Entering or exiting a building: look behind you to see

whether anyone else is coming through the same door in the next 5 seconds. If the door will slam in the face of the person behind you, hold it open.

- If you see someone right outside, and opening the door would involve no more effort than extending your arm, go ahead and give it a push.
- If there are two doors going into a building, and a large number of people are squeezing through one while the other door remains closed, open and go through the unopened door so as to optimize the flow of traffic.
- If you see someone carrying boxes, ask if there's a door you can open.

Meetings
- Don't fall asleep in meetings. Coffee or tea is your friend.
- When engaged in discussion, distinguish between criticisms of an argument and criticisms of a person.
- If you're "taking notes" on your mobile device, don't be checking personal email or non work-related websites.

Events
- If you are at a classical music performance, or in a movie theater, don't talk during the performance. Do not clap between movements, or at any point where the conductor asks you not to clap.
- What seems to be an inconspicuous whisper to you is actually quite loud, so be very cautious.
- Take off your hat.

Cell Phones
- Before entering any public meeting or event - a classroom, a library, a restaurant, a concert, a lecture, a play, or a movie, put your cell phone on vibrate or just shut it off.
- If you are waiting for an emergency call – e.g., a relative is dying – step outside and away from others to take the call.

- Be careful how loud you speak, because the tendency is to speak loud in a public place.
- Don't leave your cell phone on a table and then walk away. If it rings or vibrates, it will bother everyone, and...it compromises your personal information and security.
- If you are in a dark space with others, such as a movie, don't text-message. The light from the screen is bright and very obnoxious.

Sustainability
- If the room is empty, and you're leaving, turn off the lights.
- If you smoke and you go outside to light up, throw away your cigarette butts when you're done. Littering is not cool.
- If you have a plastic/glass/aluminum container to toss, but the nearest public recycling bin is full, hang onto it until you come to one that isn't full rather than making a pile on top of the bin.

No doubt you can add to this list, which is great. But you get the idea. Put others first and treat them well. You won't always be recognized for it, but you will contribute to the greater good of your internship site and society by these small, but significant acts of common courtesy.

 *LIFESTYLE*

You want to make the best impression possible. You want to be creative, perform assignments well, and generally be a healthy, enthusiastic worker. To do all this, you need to be at the top of your game. You need to be mentally sharp and physically healthy. Here are a few hints to keep you in top form.

Eat Well
According to WebMD, the basic components of a healthy diet include the right amount of:

- Protein (found in fish, meat, poultry, dairy products, eggs, nuts, and beans) – about 25% of your diet
- Fat (found in animal and dairy products, nuts, and oils) – about 25% of your diet
- Carbohydrates (found in fruits, vegetables, pasta, rice, grains, beans and other legumes, and sweets) – about 50% of your diet
- Vitamins (such as vitamins A, B, C, D, E, and K)
- Minerals (such as calcium, potassium, and iron)
- Water – eight 8 ounce glasses per day. The Mayo Clinic website states, "Water is your body's principal chemical component, making up, on average, 60 percent of your body weight. Every system in your body depends on water. For example, water flushes toxins out of vital organs, carries nutrients to your cells and provides a moist environment for ear, nose and throat tissues. Lack of water can lead to

dehydration, a condition that occurs when you don't have enough water in your body to carry out normal functions. Even mild dehydration can drain your energy and make you tired."

Exercise

Yes...it reduces stress, helps prevent disease, delays the aging process, and it boosts your brain power. Exercise positively affects your body and mind. A simple routine of thirty minutes of exercise per day, combined with a well-rounded diet and adherence to the other factors mentioned in this section, can do wonders for you. If you find yourself needing a quick break during your work hours, take a short walk, and/or stretch you arms, legs and back. Another simple technique is to stand at your desk and, if it won't distract anyone, do simple resistance exercises. Go to WebMD.com and search 'exercise at desk'.

Get Enough Sleep

Loss of sleep affects everything from memory to mood, working with numbers, logical reasoning, attention, and muscle dexterity. On p. 161 of his book, *Brain Rules*, Dr. John Medina writes, "What is the relationship between ordinary sleep and extraordinary learning?...Students were given a series of math problems and prepped with a method to solve them...If you let 12 hours pass after the initial training and ask the students to do more problems, about 20 percent will have discovered the shortcut. But, if in that 12 hours you also allow eight or so hours of regular sleep, that figure triples to about 60 percent." You want to perform better at work? Be sure to get seven to eight hours of sleep.

Daniel Pink writes in his book, *When: The Scientific Secrets of Perfect Timing*, that the desire to take a nap in the afternoon is not unusual. Around the world people seem to experience a low point of energy between 2:00 and 4:00 p.m. His remedy, based on science, is a "nappuccino". The ingredients?

1. Find your afternoon trough time. The Mayo clinic says the best time for a nap is between 2 and 3 p.m.
2. Create a peaceful environment. Turn off or mute your cell phone and email notifications.
3. Drink a cup of coffee. Its effect will kick in about 25 minutes later.
4. Set a timer for 25 minutes. Naps between 10 and 20 minutes boost alertness and mental function. If you nap longer, you will be groggy upon waking.
5. Repeat consistently. Habitual nappers reap better results than infrequent nappers.

Of course, you need to be cautious. At most places of employment, sleeping on the job is frowned upon or considered downright lazy. Maybe you can help change the workplace culture by finding ways to introduce Daniel Pink's advice to your supervisor and co-workers, since it is based on scientific research.

Keep Your Emotional State Free and Clear
Trying to meet deadlines, deal with irate customers and challenging colleagues, overtime issues, cutbacks, and more contribute to a build-up of stress, which can literally ravage your immune system. It can kill white blood cells. Sickness, disease, and impaired brain functioning can result from it.

All of the lifestyle issues mentioned above will help you deal with stress, but there is another resource that will help. Keep yourself emotionally healthy. One way to do that is to not harbor a grudge, maintain a resentful attitude towards someone else, or try to get even.

Meditate
Find a comfortable chair and relax. Put a pen and notepad next to you. Play some soft, relaxing music (without lyrics). Start by concentrating on your breathing. Close your eyes and imagine

yourself in a peaceful place.

If distracting thoughts enter into your mind, acknowledge them. If tasks come to mind, such as something you need to do in the office, or an item you need to get on the way back to your apartment, write them down and re-focus on your breathing. You don't need to empty your mind. You can focus on aspects of the peaceful place you have chosen (a lake, a forest, the ocean, the mountains, or a room from your childhood), or you can choose a proverb to contemplate, such as the following:

- "The heaviest ear of corn bows its head the lowest." (Irish)
- "One hand can't tie a bundle." (Basa)
- "The one who is not hungry calls the coconut shells hard." (Ethiopian)
- "When friends are together, even water is sweet." (Chinese)
- "He who walks with the wise grows wise, but a companion of fools suffers harm." (Jewish)

Meditate for five to ten minutes to start. You may wish to go longer as you continue the practice. It's completely up to you.

CRITICAL THINKING/PROBLEM SOLVING

One of the primary skills you need to develop as a professional is how to think critically and solve problems. If you follow the steps below and develop this skill for issues that arise during your internship, you will make yourself invaluable to any organization.

"Skilled, active, interpretation and evaluation of observations, communications, information and argumentation" is one way to define critical thinking. It helps us to identify, analyze, and evaluate information presented to us, in order to come to logical, rational conclusions. It provides us with the tools we need to make good decisions.

1. Identify and Define
   a. Is there, indeed, an actual problem?
   b. If so, it needs to be clearly delineated.
2. Gather Facts
   a. Use the six key questions - who, what, when, where, why, and how – to ascertain facts such as statistics, time factors, and history
   b. Contact all parties involved to gain their perspective and understanding
   c. Separate facts from feelings, opinions, attitudes, personality conflicts, gossip, and intuition
3. Identify the Root Cause
   a. Is this an issue with a personality, process, or pro-

cedure?

    b. Did a combination of factors come into play?

4. Brainstorm Possible Solutions

    a. No idea is stupid; judgment on ideas is reserved until after a list is developed

    b. Consider taking two or more ideas and melding them together for a possible solution

    c. Be sure to check out the chapter on Creativity

5. Narrow List to the Best Solutions

    a. "Best" solutions will effectively resolve the issue at hand with the least amount of disruption to the department or organization and the least harm done to an individual or group

6. Evaluate Solutions

    a. What are the pros and cons of each?

    b. What resources, human or otherwise, are needed to successfully implement each?

7. Implement Final Solution

    a. Who will be responsible for carrying out the solution?

    b. What is the detailed procedure for implementation?

    c. What is the timeline?

    d. Clearly communicate solution to all parties concerned

OFFICE ROMANCE

During the course of your internship, you may encounter one or more people for whom you develop an attraction, or who may be attracted to you. There are several points you need to consider, however, before you pursue those feelings. Workplace relationships need to be thought through. Let's go down a list of positive and negative aspects.

Positive
- If you work with a person on a somewhat regular basis, you gain some understanding of their likes/dislikes and lifestyle preferences.
- You may enjoy the smiles, the playful jokes, breaks and meals together, and secret emails or notes.
- Finding someone to hang out with at departmental or organization events is no longer an issue.

Negative
- You may be violating a stated policy of the organization.
- Your email may be monitored or used against you in the future.
- You can stir feelings of jealousy with other co-workers.
- Others will no longer view you as a "neutral" party in discussions or work on projects, especially if both of you are in the same group. They may perceive you as a "voting block" of two.
- If there is a disruption in your relationship, it will add stress

to both your lives and will make it all the harder for you to focus on the work at hand.

• Instead of just seeing and hearing your ideas, people may begin to blur the two of you into one. Your identity may be somewhat lost.

• If it is your boss with whom a relationship is growing, you risk even greater alienation from co-workers. Among other things, they will see favoritism in every action and decision the boss makes.

• The relationship may have a negative impact on a potential job with the organization or with obtaining letters of reference.

• Your internship may be terminated, and/or the one in whom you are interested may be terminated.

Close friendships are fine, but go no further. The bottom line - the safe path is to forego any love relationship during your internship.

EXPERIENCE A MID-LIFE CRISIS NOW!

A mid-life crisis is a phenomenon you may have observed in recent years in a family member. This occurs primarily in the 30-50 year-old age range, and it can happen more than once. It is often characterized by a person waking up one day and saying, "Why am I doing what I'm doing? I have always wanted to _____." Then, in extreme cases where they don't know how to handle the feelings well, an individual may go out and buy a new car, or go on an extravagant spending spree, or leave their job and spouse for someone and/or something else.

So, what does this have to do with you in your internship? Well...why go through an experience like that? Is it inevitable? More than once in your career you will feel dissatisfaction with work. It seems that an issue such as this can be addressed earlier in your career – like right now. Here is a little exercise. Think about the following questions and how you would answer them.

1. If you had no restrictions on money, time, geographical location, approval of parents or a significant other, or what your major is, what would you really like to do down deep in your heart?

2. What resources (family, friends, acquaintances, training, financial, etc.) do you have which may allow you to enjoy that dream job/career?

3. What tangible steps can you take towards that goal? Write down the steps and due dates for each one. Remember

goals without deadlines are just wisps of a dream.

There was a student who went through this exercise and concluded she wanted to be, or at least try being, a hot air balloon pilot. She was encouraged to first go up in a balloon to see if she even enjoyed the experience. A couple months later she met a young man whose father owned a hot air balloon company. She asked many questions and got a better feel for the business end of things. Then, for a birthday present, she was given a ride. She loved it!

Don't put off your dream. Look for ways to nourish it.

After the information interviews and her first ride, she reflected on what is involved with ballooning and decided that, for now, she would focus on graduate school and a career that would offer better compensation. But she still holds out the possibility that, one day, she will pilot a hot air balloon. The important thing is she at least got a taste of her dream job.

Don't put off your dream. Look for ways to nourish it. For example, if you dream of traveling the world, but money or circumstances currently hinder you, stream travel videos, especially those that delve into a country's culture. Be sure to read books, blogs, and newspapers about geographical areas of interest. Look for ways to connect with international students from these countries. All of these learning opportunities will enhance your experience when you actually get to your destination.

Also, look into *Designing Your Life* by Burnett and Evans - https://designingyour.life - and *What Should I Do With My Life?* by Po Bronson.

 *ENDING WELL*

Ending your internship well is just as important as beginning it well. It is a matter of integrity. Remember, too, it is a small world. You need to understand the people you leave behind may cross your path again in the future. You may need their assistance, so try to exit with grace and on good terms with your co-workers.

Make sure you DO these things:
- Maintain your level of productivity right up to the end.
- Bring closure to as many work projects/assignments as possible. For incomplete or ongoing projects, organize them in such a way that someone else can easily continue them.
- Offer to brief your successor in any way possible, even by responding to phone calls after you have left.
- Bring closure to your work relationships. Say good-bye to anyone with whom you had close contact, both inside and outside the organization. Let them know why and when you are leaving.
- Learn if your supervisor(s), if asked in the future, are willing to provide references about your work.
- Find a meaningful way to say "thank you". Think about those who were helpful to you when you began your internship and while you worked there. This may be as simple as writing a thank you note, bringing in handmade food, or buying some flowers to brighten the area.

Make sure you DO NOT:
- Become casual in the last days of your internship, either by the way you dress or the way in which you work.
- Turn into a management consultant and criticize your present organization, especially in writing.
- Pass on to your successor negative thoughts about your organization or individuals who work in it. You don't know them or what work they may be given. They may have a completely different experience from yours.
- Go around and "tell off" those who made your life difficult. Who knows? Some day those very persons may turn out to be your boss, colleague or customer.
- Promise to stay in touch, unless you really mean it and plan to follow through.

TRANSLATING EXPERIENCES FOR EMPLOYERS

You are fluent in at least one language other than your native tongue. Did you know that? You speak the language of your experiences and background. It is a rich language with a vocabulary all its own. But others cannot understand it because it is unique to you. This requires use of a special skill you also possess, but is largely unused.

Because of your fluency in the language of your experiences, you now need to use the skill of interpretation. Translating your unique experiences helps others understand all you have learned. When you do this for employers, they better understand how your abilities fit in with what they need.

Consider first where we often see or hear of translators being involved: meetings between world leaders one-on-one or at group events like the G7 conferences; global sports events such as the Olympics or World Cup soccer; and, of course, at the United Nations General Assembly in New York City. Translation takes place between businesses, in healthcare clinics, in book publishing, and in many other settings.

Two famous translation gaffes took place during the visit of U.S. President Jimmy Carter to Poland in 1977. During a speech to the Polish people the President said, "when I left the United States," but the translation came out as "when I abandoned the

United States." The one getting the biggest laugh, however, was when he mentioned "your desires for the future." The people heard the interpreter say "your lusts for the future." Translation, as you can see, calls for getting not just the words but the nuances and ideas of a language correct.

So, how do you communicate your experiences in a way that others, especially employers, clearly understand? Your skill as an interpreter should be clearly revealed in print, as on a resume or LinkedIn profile, and verbally in a job interview.

- First, read the job or industry description carefully. What skills or experiences are required for a successful candidate? Create a list of these using language directly from the position description.
- Second, identify your strengths and the skills you already possess and lay them out in a second list. If you have not yet purchased the book *StrengthsFinder* by Tom Rath and have not taken the Gallup strengths online assessment which comes with the book, you should.
- Third, look at your life experiences, including your internships, college projects, sports, clubs, work-study positions, and off-campus employment, among others. Reflect on what you learned, not just what you did, and write it down in a third list.
- Fourth, take time to look across the three lists you have created. Compare them. Where do your skills and learning from experience match what the organization has posted?

Certainly, your discipline-specific or "hard" skills will be necessary, but more often than not, it is your soft skills that will be the added weight which tips the scales in your favor. These may include project management, communication, data analysis, and leadership.

Examples

- History Department Work-Study
  - ○ Currently on resume'
    - ▪ Assisted department chair with event
    - ▪ Posted current information to department blog
  - ○ Newly translated version
    - ▪ Learned how to plan and execute a successful History Scholars event by managing multiple contacts and venues, both on and off-campus
    - ▪ Researched, analyzed, and identified appropriate content for blog
    - ▪ Archived blog content in Pocket app and then posted using Wix
- Course Project
  - ○ Currently on resume'
    - ▪ Worked with student team on water purification system
    - ▪ Successfully completed project
  - ○ Newly translated version
    - ▪ Articulated strategic goals for student team
    - ▪ Implemented timelines to measure progress
    - ▪ Oversaw budget of $7,000
    - ▪ Made sure final deliverable was completed according to specifications
- Internship
  - ○ Currently on resume'
    - ▪ Helped non-profit sports organization to improve services
    - ▪ Provided management with requested information
  - ○ Newly translated version
    - ▪ Observed activities firsthand at various branches
    - ▪ Recorded measurable numbers for activities in Excel
    - ▪ Analyzed activities by day, time, clientele, and lo-

cation using a pivot table
- Developed an executive summary with recommendations for future marketing efforts
- Study Abroad
  - Currently on resume'
    - Took courses at local university
    - Visited several sites in country
  - Newly translated version
    - Solved problem of fastest route between three locations and navigated transportation system in large urban area
    - Communicated with faculty and general populace in their native tongue
    - Incorporated nuances in speech and increased my translation speed
    - Enhanced my cultural appreciation through stay with host family
    - Learned procedures/processes through job shadowing experiences with businesses and non-profit organizations

PERSONAL BRANDING AND TRANSITIONING TO EMPLOYMENT

After seeing you in action during the semester, your employer may offer you a position at the conclusion of the internship. If so, congratulations! Unless you choose to look for employment elsewhere, you are set. If your internship employer has not offered you full-time employment, you have work to do.

First, you need to consider your personal brand. You are your own salesperson. It is up to you to market yourself as best you can with all of the human and technological resources available to you.

Think about a visual identity. This could be a use of certain colors, a graphic element, and/or a set of descriptive words on your professional card, resume, and website. Whatever you choose to incorporate, be sure the components communicate something significant about who you are and what you want to do.

Here are some ideas to assist you in your transition to full-time employment.

Update Your Resume
All internship and work experiences should be listed in reverse chronological order, with your internship displayed at the top of the list. Be sure to include new skills you acquired during

your experience. Be sure to use bullet points with action verbs like: assisted, acquired, tested, supervised, researched, embedded, wrote, managed, planned, etc.

Secure References
Talk with select individuals who know your work the best. Ask professors, your internship supervisor, and work supervisors if they would be willing to serve as references for you. You may wish to ask them for letters of reference which you can scan and upload to your website (see below) and which you may show to individuals at your job interviews.

Create A Portfolio
Hopefully you have documented the projects on which you have worked. Samples may include documents you have created or contributed to: newsletters, web-based articles, social media updates, photos, graphs, screen shots of spreadsheets, reflective narratives, and so on.

Note: Be sure your internship site supervisor reviews all materials before you include them in a paper or electronic version of the portfolio. He/she will want to be sure no confidential information is shared.

Market Yourself Online
Create an online portfolio for free and upload your samples - pdf documents, website links, photos, and movies. Check out free sites such as:

Wix – wix.com
Duda – duda.co
Weebly – weebly.com
Strikingly – strikingly.com

LinkedIn.com

If you have not already created an online profile using LinkedIn, do it today! This service is quickly becoming the defacto resume and global, professional networking resource for women and men. After you create an account, it will automatically generate a weblink with your name. This becomes part of your digital presence.

Prepare Yourself

Review websites related to interviewing (especially behavior-based) and the job search process, including evaluating and negotiating job offers and benefit plans.

Initiate and Persist

Getting yourself and your material (resume, references, and portfolio) ready is crucial, but then you need to research organizations, make contacts, apply, follow-up, and…persist.

Daniel Pink in his book, *To Sell Is Human*, writes on p. 119: "When something bad occurs, ask yourself three questions – and come up with an intelligent way to answer each one 'no':

6. Is this permanent?

    Bad Response: 'Yes. I've completely lost my skill for moving others.'

    Better Response: 'No. I was flat today because I haven't been getting enough sleep.'

7. Is this pervasive?

    Bad Response: 'Yes. Everyone in this industry is impossible to deal with.'

    Better Response: 'No. This particular guy was a jerk.'

8. Is this personal?

    Bad Response: 'Yes. The reason he didn't buy (or hire me) is that I messed up my presentation.'

    Better Response: 'No. My presentation could have been better, but the real reason he passed is that he wasn't ready to buy right now.'

The more you explain bad events as *temporary, specific,* and *external,* the more likely you are to persist even in the face of adversity."

The job search process is seldom easy. You need to consistently and patiently move forward.

Best wishes on your journey!

QUICK NOTES – DINING ETIQUETTE

- Turn off cell phone, or place on vibrate, and keep it out-of-sight
- Nametag goes on upper right lapel
- Turn name place card around for others at your table to see
- Key off your host/hostess
- Remove napkin from table when your host/hostess does
- Order mid-price range or ask your host for suggestions
- Don't order messy foods like spaghetti
- Place Setting - looking left to right - BMW - Bread Plate, Main Dish, Water (see illustration below)
- Utensils - work from the outside in
- Don't start to eat until everyone at your table has been served
- Bread - tear off one piece at a time and butter it
- Cut food two pieces at a time and eat
- Pass salt and pepper together, never just one (same applies to sugar and cream)
- Don't talk with food in your mouth
- Don't blow your nose at the table
- Don't pick your teeth at the table
- Conversation - be aware of local, national, and international news
- Conversation - stay away from controversial subjects
- Take business cards to share

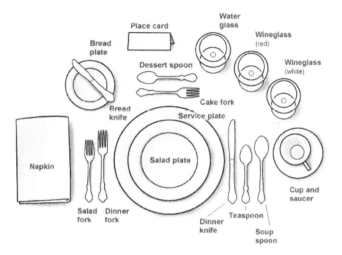

QUICK NOTES – CONDUCTING A MEETING

- Be sure there is a clear purpose
- Set a specific time and length of time to meet
- Plan for appropriate meeting space and equipment
- Send an agenda (with purpose, time, and place) one day before and the day of
- Take notes – written, electronic, or recorded
- Specific action items and assignments should be made (and noted in the minutes)
- Set a day and time for the next meeting, only if one is needed
- Condense notes and send out minutes within two days

BLOURNAL
QUESTIONS FOR REFLECTION

Blournaling (blogging/journaling) is a proven learning tool because it provides a structured attempt at observation and reflection. Reflective journaling assists you in focusing upon, recording, and cataloging your observations. It will also serve as a catalyst for processing thoughts and feelings regarding the new people and circumstances you are encountering. Reflection is a doorway to deeper learning. The tools you use to record your reflections, whether paper-based or digital, are up to you. Your advisor may want you to post them on the learning management system used at your school.

1. First Impressions
What observations can you make about your internship site and its people? What appeals to you? What feelings are you experiencing? What has been your greatest challenge in the first couple weeks?

2. Organizational Mission
Identify the mission or purpose of your internship organization. In order to help you do this assignment effectively, interview one or several coworkers. Ask them to explain what they understand the mission of the organization to be. Indicate what resources or people you consulted.

Explain what you have come to understand as the mission of the organization. Besides earning a profit or providing a service, why does it exist? What is unique about its product or service, especially when compared to competitors or similar organizations? How might this understanding of organizational mission influence your approach to your internship duties?

3. Organizational Structure

Obtain a copy of an organizational chart with positions, departments, lines of authority, etc. If none exists, develop a chart based on your observations. Indicate your position on the chart. Consider your internship site and coworkers.

Who seems to have power and influence? Who makes things happen? Who has commanded your respect and why? Who has the respect of others? Is it the same person? Compare your observations with the official organizational chart. Does the organizational chart truly reflect what you are observing regarding authority and influence? Are there any political strategies that you should, or should not, engage in?

4. Management Philosophy

This section ties into your reflection on organizational structure. Does your organization have a hierarchical structure (CEO or Executive Director, with a list of personnel under them in a top-down arrangement) or more of a flat structure (a leader or co-leaders, but more of a mentality that everyone is equal)? Are issues processed for long periods of time, or is there a quicker "identify – assess – problem solve" mentality? How are decisions made?

5. Supervisor and Subordinates

Many factors can influence your work environment and productivity. Your understanding of, and relation to, your work supervisor can help you accomplish more during your time at the site.

What do you know about your supervisor? What do you know about your supervisor's relationship with his or her subordinates? For instance, do they talk to their subordinates frequently? Does your supervisor socialize with subordinates? Does your supervisor prefer a formal or informal style of communication?

6. Supervisor's Priorities

Consider the supervisor's agenda. What are the highest priorities for your supervisor? What are his or her key objectives? What is his or her definition of excellent performance? What does your supervisor expect of you?

7. Supervisor's Qualities and Style

What is your supervisor's peak time of day? What are his or her mood cycles? Work habits? What are your supervisor's strengths and weaknesses?

8. Supervisor's External Influences

Do NOT ask your supervisor these questions. Answers are to be gathered from observation. These questions are intended for you to better understand your supervisor as a whole person.

What kind of relationship does your supervisor have with his or her supervisor? Is your supervisor involved in community organizations? Is your supervisor involved with a community sports team? Do they have a hobby? Is your supervisor married? Does he or she have children? Elderly parents? What religion does your supervisor espouse? Do they seek to bring their faith into the workplace?

9. Role Models

Who is known within the organization as an ethical, value-based leader? What qualities or characteristics do people see in her or him? What have you observed?

10. Office Politics

Have you observed "political" situations in your work area? ("Political" in this context has nothing to do with whether a person is Democrat, Republican, or has some other party affiliation.) What person or group holds power? Is your supervisor a politically sensitive individual? Who are your supervisor's friends? Enemies?

11. Working for a Non-Profit Organization

If you work for a non-profit, how does it receive funding? Is it through memberships, or grants, or special events, or private donations, or a combination of these? How do businesses and/or government agencies interact with your site? Do they assist your non-profit with services, events, or funding? Do you feel the organization takes an effective, appropriate approach to sources of funding and other resources? What, in your opinion, could be changed to make the organization more effective in its mission?

12. Service

Have you found ways to incorporate service into your internship? Does your organization support a particular non-profit, or do they offer time off for community service projects? Are individuals or departments rewarded for service activities? Is there a point person for service-related activities in your organization or department? How does your organization's commitment to service, or the lack of it, affect you?

13. Professionalism

Based on your observations and experience, how would you define "professionalism" for the career field in which you are interested? What behaviors and attitudes do you believe are essential to being a professional? What examples of good or poor professionalism have you experienced or observed? How does professional behavior differ from behavior as a student? How is your own professional style emerging? What changes are you seeing in yourself? In what ways do you want to improve, develop, or refine your own professional style?

14. Career Exploration

Identify someone either within your organization or outside, who represents a profession or occupation you find appealing or are simply curious about. Schedule a time to meet with that person and conduct an information interview. Afterwards, send a thank you note to the interviewee. Who did you interview? Provide their name, title and date. Why did you select this person? What did you learn? What new insights did you gain about a particular profession or occupation? What issues create excitement, or concern, as you consider your particular career?

15. Belief System

The following questions deal with faith. If you do not subscribe to any traditional expression of faith in God, what are your core values? Use those core values to answer the following questions.

What role, if any, does your faith play in your internship and career choice? Do you believe your faith should be an intricate part of your daily work, or do you feel it should be separate from your work? In what ways do you think culture has influenced your perspective on faith and work?

16. Ethics

Ethics according to the Merriam-Webster Dictionary is "the discipline dealing with what is good and bad and with moral duty and obligation; a set of moral principles." What ethical issues, or violations of good moral behavior, are you most likely to encounter in your profession? What values and convictions do you bring to the marketplace? In what ways can you expect coworkers to react to you because of those values? What character traits would you most want to be remembered for in your internship or career by others?

17. Transferable Skills

In the years ahead it will not be your academic major that secures you a job and allows you to keep it. Most likely the transferable skills you possess will be the deciding factor.

Visit at least three websites (one should be from outside your home country), which talk about transferable skills. List the web addresses of the sites. Compare differences in definitions and lists of skills, identify your own transferable skills, and provide an analysis of how you use those skills in your current internship. Finally, write how you plan to develop skills in your areas of weakness.

18. Concluding Your Experience

As your internship or co-op experience comes to a conclusion, what do you feel have been your major accomplishments? What new skills or abilities have you gained? Discuss at least two areas of personal or professional growth.

 **WEB RESOURCES**

InternQube.com has a multitude of resources to help you further develop your professional skills. Check out the weblinks, videos, articles, book recommendations, and more.